Randomness

The Hidden Force Behind AI's Success

Fang Li, PhD

First Edition: December 2024

To my family,
who make everything possible

"The lot is cast into the lap,
but its every decision is from the Lord."

— Proverbs 16:33

Contents

Epilogue

Glossary of Terms

Preface: When being wrong feels right

As a computer science professor specializing in explainable AI, I spent years looking down on deep learning. "It's just a black box," I would tell my students, wearing my skepticism like a badge of honor. "How can we trust something we don't understand?"

In every semester, I posed this scenario to my classes: Imagine you're a soldier in a warzone, choosing between two robot partners. The first runs on traditional, rule-based AI – you can inspect every decision-making rule, trace every action it would take. The second runs on deep learning – far more capable in practice, but its decision-making process is largely opaque. Which would you trust with your life?

The answer seemed obvious to me. Until it wasn't.

My journey from skeptic to believer wasn't sudden – it was more like watching a photograph develop in a darkroom, the image slowly emerging from darkness. It began with a mathematical revelation that shook my understanding of artificial intelligence to its core. I was studying word embeddings, a technique where AI represents words as points in a vast mathematical space, when I discovered something that left me speechless.

Take the word "bike" and subtract "car" – the resulting mathematical distance was surprisingly meaningful. Compare that to "bike" minus "cat," and the distance was much larger. The AI had somehow captured the inherent relationship between transportation methods, without ever being explicitly taught these categories.

Even more astonishing: take "Moscow," subtract "Russia," and you get almost exactly the same mathematical relationship as "Beijing" minus "China." Through exposure to vast amounts of text, these AI systems had discovered fundamental relationships about our world – relationships we never programmed, patterns we never taught.

This was my first glimpse into a profound truth: maybe some aspects of intelligence simply can't be explained through explicit rules. Just as we humans can't truly visualize a four-dimensional object (though we can work with it mathematically), perhaps there are aspects of intelligence that resist being broken down into neat, explainable components.

Then came ChatGPT. Its ability to engage in nuanced

conversation, understand context, and generate human-like responses forced me to confront my long-held beliefs. Here was a system that worked precisely because it embraced uncertainty, because it wasn't bound by rigid rules of what language should be.

I began to see that my insistence on explainability had been like trying to catch water with a net. In our quest to make AI understandable, had we been holding it back? After all, we humans often can't explain how we know what we know. Ask an expert chef why they added just that pinch of spice at just that moment, or a veteran doctor how they spotted a subtle diagnosis – they might struggle to articulate their reasoning, even as they know with certainty they're right.

This book is about that journey – from the quest for perfect explainability to the recognition that randomness and uncertainty might be essential components of intelligence, not flaws to be eliminated. It's about how embracing the unknown led to some of the most significant breakthroughs in artificial intelligence.

And yes, I've revised my answer about that robot soldier. Because sometimes, just like with human partners, the ability to perform in complex, unpredictable situations matters more than being able to explain every decision. Sometimes, our quest for perfect explainability can be the very thing that holds us back from deeper understanding.

In the following chapters, we'll explore why randomness isn't just a feature of intelligent systems – it might be a requirement. We'll see how nature uses randomness to create complexity, how uncertainty drives learning, and why the future of AI might depend on our willingness to embrace what we can't fully explain.

Welcome to the paradox where being less certain can make us more capable, where accepting our limitations can lead to our greatest breakthroughs, and where randomness might just be the hidden force behind artificial intelligence we've been seeking all along.

A note to my readers: This book isn't meant to be a rigorous academic publication. Rather, it's a personal narrative of my discoveries about randomness, uncertainty, and artificial intelligence during my years of research and teaching. I'm sharing my thoughts and experiences as someone who has both witnessed and participated in the evolution of AI, but I'm also acutely aware of my own limitations. There may be mistakes, oversights, or areas where my understanding falls short – and for these, I apologize in advance. My goal isn't to present definitive answers, but to invite you into the fascinating journey of questioning our assumptions about intelligence, both artificial and human.

Fang Li

Dec, 2024

The Paradox of Intelligence

Why perfect logic fails in real world

In 1997, something remarkable happened: a computer beat the world chess champion. Many thought this meant artificial intelligence was on the verge of matching human capabilities. After all, if a machine could master chess – one of humanity's most complex games – surely everything else would follow? Yet decades later, robots still struggle with tasks any five-year-old can do, like reliably picking up toys or understanding simple jokes.

You know what's funny? We've been here before. Back in the 1950s, a bunch of brilliant scientists got together and made a bold prediction: they claimed we'd soon have machines that could think just like humans. They were so confident! "Give us a generation," they said, "and computers will be chatting with us, making art, and discovering new scientific theories." One famous researcher even declared that within twenty years, machines would be able to do any job a human could do.

Why were they so optimistic? Well, they'd just created some pretty impressive programs. One could solve mathematical proofs (and even found a better solution than some famous mathematicians!). Another seemed to understand human conversation, though it was really just playing a clever matching game with words. These early successes made them think they'd cracked the code of human intelligence.

But here's the thing: real intelligence isn't like solving math problems or following logical rules. Think about how you recognize your friend's face in a crowd. You're not measuring the distance between their eyes or calculating the angle of their nose – you just look and know. Or when you're driving and you notice a kid on a bike looking like they might swerve into your lane. You're not running physics calculations – you just naturally adjust your driving.

Let me share a story that really shows this difference. In the 1980s, Japan spent billions trying to build computers that could understand language and interpret pictures. They had the best researchers, the most advanced technology, and a clear plan: break everything down into logical rules, just like solving a math problem. Want to guess how it turned out? Despite all that money and brainpower, they couldn't even come close to matching what your brain does effortlessly every day.

Here's a perfect example of what I mean: imagine you're in a car factory in the 1980s. They've got these impressive robots that can install windshields with perfect precision, never getting tired or complaining about backaches. Sounds great, right? But watch what happens when something unexpected occurs – say, a cracked windshield comes down the line. A human worker would notice immediately and stop. The robot? It just keeps going through its programmed motions, sometimes causing thousands of dollars in damage. It's following its logic perfectly, but missing the common sense that any human would have.

And speaking of seeing things, here's a funny story from the early days of computer vision. Back in 1966, a professor at MIT thought teaching computers to see would be a nice summer project for his students. Just connect a camera to a computer and have it describe what it sees – how hard could it be? Well, we're still working on that "summer project" decades later! It turns out that seeing isn't just about detecting edges and shapes, like those early researchers thought.

Think about how you see the world. When you look at a cat, are you mentally calculating geometric shapes and edge patterns? Of course not! You just see a cat. Even better, you can recognize a cat in a child's crayon drawing, or a cartoon, or even just a few lines scratched in the sand. Try explaining to a computer what makes all those different images "cat-like" using pure logic – it's nearly impossible!

The story gets even better when we talk about language. Back during the Cold War, people thought computer translation would be simple. Just give the computer a dictionary and some grammar rules, right? Well, they tried translating "The spirit is willing but the flesh is weak" into Russian and back. Want to know what they got? "The vodka is good but the meat is rotten." I'm not making this up! It's a perfect example of how language isn't just about following rules – it's about understanding context and meaning.

Even today's fanciest AI language systems, impressive as they are, sometimes say things that a five-year-old would know are nonsense. They'll happily write stories about skiing on the ocean or cooking with sunshine because they're just playing with words – they don't really understand what these things mean in the real world.

Let's talk about self-driving cars – now there's a humbling story! In 2004, the government offered a million-dollar prize for any self-driving car that could complete a 150-mile desert course. Simple enough, right? Just follow the path, don't hit anything. Every single car failed. The next year, after tons more work, five cars finally finished. Everyone got excited, predicting we'd all have self-driving cars within a decade. Well, it's 2024 now, and we're still waiting.

Why is it so hard? Because driving isn't just about following traffic rules and recognizing stop signs. Think about all the little judgments you make while driving: that pedestrian is looking at their phone and might step out; that truck ahead is swaying slightly, maybe the driver is tired; that patch of road looks wet and might be slippery. You process all of this automatically, without even realizing you're doing it.

This reminds me of some fascinating research done with firefighters. Researchers wanted to understand how fire captains make those split-second, life-or-death decisions. They expected to find that these experts were rapidly analyzing situations and weighing options. But that's not what happened at all. When asked how they knew a building was about to collapse, experienced firefighters would say things like, "It just didn't feel right" or "Something about the smoke looked wrong." They couldn't explain their reasoning with logical rules – they just knew.

You see this same pattern everywhere you look. Watch a master chef cooking without a recipe, adjusting everything by taste and feel. Or a skilled nurse who knows a patient is in trouble before any machines start beeping. Or a veteran mechanic who can diagnose an engine problem just by listening to it. These experts aren't following a mental checklist – they're drawing on patterns they've learned through years of experience.

In the 1980s, people tried to capture this expertise in computer programs called expert systems. The idea was simple: interview the experts, write down their rules, and put those rules in a computer. Sometimes it worked okay for very specific tasks, but it always ran into the same problem: the real world is messier than any set of rules can handle.

Take XCON, a computer system designed to configure computer systems for Digital Equipment Corporation. At first, everyone thought it was a huge success. But they kept having to add more and more rules to handle different situations. The system grew from 2,500 rules to over 10,000 in just a few years. And the more rules they added, the more likely it was to break when it encountered something slightly new.

But human intelligence doesn't break that way. We're amazingly good at handling new situations. A chef can work with ingredients they've never seen before. A teacher can explain the same concept ten different ways based on what works for each student. A basketball player can adapt their strategy on the fly when the opponent does something unexpected.

Looking back at the history of AI, it seems like we've been coming at this all wrong. We started with things that seemed to require intelligence – like playing chess or solving logic puzzles – and assumed that's what intelligence is all about. But maybe real intelligence is more about dealing with uncertainty and adapting to new situations than about following logical rules.

This tells us something really important about our own intelligence. Those qualities that make human intelligence special – our flexibility, our intuition, our ability to understand context – come from our ability to go beyond rigid rules. We can break the rules when we need to, trust our gut feelings, and adapt when things don't quite fit our expectations.

It doesn't mean we'll never create artificial intelligence. But it does suggest we need to think differently about how we do it. Instead of trying to write perfect rules for everything, maybe we need to focus more on how humans actually learn and adapt.

And here's a thought: maybe this understanding can help us be better at developing human capabilities too. Instead of trying to reduce everything to rigid rules and procedures, we could focus more on helping people develop their intuition and pattern-recognition skills. After all, the most sophisticated forms of human intelligence often come from knowing when to break the rules, not just how to follow them.

The limits of human understanding (4D example)

Imagine you're teaching a child about shapes. Point, line, square, cube – each step adds a new dimension, and it all makes perfect sense. Now try this: close your eyes and imagine a four-dimensional cube. Not the mathematical formula, not a computer rendering, but really see it in your mind, as clearly as you can picture a regular cube on your desk.

Impossible, right? Don't worry – even Einstein couldn't do it. And here's where it gets interesting: this limitation tells us something crucial about artificial intelligence.

Let's try a simple exercise together. Start with a point – just a dot, zero dimensions. Easy. Now stretch that point into a line – one dimension. Pull that line sideways to create a square – two dimensions. Lift that square "up" to create a cube – three dimensions. Following along so far? Good. Now for the mind-bender: try to pull that cube in a fourth spatial direction, one that's perpendicular to length, width, and height.

Your brain probably just short-circuited a bit. Mine does too, every time. This is exactly the kind of barrier that AI systems hit when dealing with real-world complexity. Just as our brains are wired for a three-dimensional world and struggle with the fourth dimension, traditional AI is wired for perfect logic and struggles with the messy, multidimensional nature of reality.

This isn't about intelligence or education. The world's top mathematicians can write equations describing four-dimensional space all day long. They can calculate its properties with perfect precision. But ask them to visualize it? They're just as stuck as we are. Similarly, AI can process vast amounts of data and perform complex calculations, but it stumbles when faced with tasks requiring genuine understanding or adaptation.

Think about what this means. We humans pride ourselves on our ability to understand anything if we try hard enough. We've split atoms, mapped the human genome, and sent robots to Mars. Yet we can't visualize something as simple as a four-dimensional cube. Our minds, incredible as they are, have built-in limits. These limits aren't bugs – they're features that shape how we think and solve problems.

The limits are everywhere once you start looking. Try to invent a new color – not orange or purple, but a completely new color you've never seen before. Try to truly grasp infinity, not just as a concept but as a reality. Try to picture quantum particles existing in multiple states simultaneously without resorting to metaphors like Schrödinger's cat. Each of these mental barriers is like a window into how our intelligence actually works.

Even everyday tasks reveal our brain's boundaries. Try keeping track of more than seven things at once. Try creating a truly random sequence of numbers (computers analyze human-generated "random" numbers precisely because we're so bad at being random). Try deliberately forgetting your phone number for five minutes. These limitations might seem like weaknesses, but they're actually part of what makes human intelligence so remarkable.

Here's where it gets fascinating. Despite these mental limits – or maybe because of them – we've accomplished remarkable things. We've developed mathematics that describes dimensions we can never see. We've built quantum computers that harness principles we can't intuitively understand. We've created technologies that would seem like magic to our ancestors. Our inability to fully grasp these concepts hasn't stopped us from using them effectively.

This is where current AI approaches often miss the mark. They try to achieve intelligence through perfect logic and unlimited processing power, but human intelligence works differently. We're more like jazz musicians than calculators – we improvise, adapt, and work around our limitations in creative ways.

It's like we've built mental tools specifically to reach beyond our mind's limitations. We can't visualize four dimensions, but we can describe them with mathematics. We can't intuitively grasp quantum mechanics, but we can use it to build new technologies. We can't directly perceive most of the electromagnetic spectrum, but we've built devices that can. In each case, we've found ways to transcend our cognitive limits rather than trying to break through them directly.

This hints at something profound about both human and artificial intelligence. Maybe our inability to fully understand certain things isn't a flaw – it's a crucial feature. Maybe intelligence isn't about having unlimited mental capacity or perfect logical reasoning, but about finding clever ways to transcend our limitations.

Think about it: a fish doesn't need to understand hydrodynamics to swim beautifully. A baseball player doesn't need to solve differential equations to catch a fly ball. Perhaps our conscious mind's inability to fully understand how we do complex things – from recognizing faces to learning languages – isn't a failure. Perhaps it's an essential part of how intelligence works. And maybe this is exactly what we're missing in our attempts to create artificial intelligence.

This brings us to a beautiful irony: the very thing we're trying to understand – intelligence – might be, by its nature, something that cannot be fully understood by intelligence itself. It's like trying to use a ruler to measure its own length, or a camera to photograph itself without using mirrors. Just as we can't visualize four dimensions but can work with them mathematically, maybe we can't fully comprehend intelligence but can still find ways to recreate it.

As we continue exploring the nature of intelligence and our attempts to recreate it artificially, this paradox offers an important lesson. The limits of our understanding aren't obstacles to be overcome – they're crucial clues about what intelligence really is. Instead of trying to build AI systems that transcend all limitations through pure logic, perhaps we should be designing systems that, like human intelligence, work brilliantly within and around their constraints.

First hint: maybe unexplainability is necessary

Let's consider a radical idea: What if the mysterious, unexplainable parts of our intelligence aren't bugs, but features? What if some things about intelligence have to be unexplainable for it to work at all? This might sound strange, but stay with me – it could change how we think about both human and artificial intelligence.

Picture this: You're at a busy airport, scanning hundreds of faces in the crowd. Suddenly, you spot your friend. The recognition is instant, automatic, certain. Now try to explain exactly how you did that. Which features did you check? What was the precise sequence of steps? You can't say, can you? Your smartphone does something remarkably similar when it unlocks after recognizing your face. Just like you, it doesn't follow a simple checklist like "check nose shape, then eye color, then hair." Instead, it processes the whole face at once, in ways that even its programmers don't fully understand.

This parallel between human and artificial intelligence is everywhere in our daily lives. When you ask Siri or Alexa a question, they understand you despite different accents, background noise, or ways of phrasing – just like humans do. Neither can explain exactly how they decode the sound waves into meaningful words.

When Netflix suggests a show you might like, it's doing something similar to how you recommend movies to friends – picking up on patterns you can't quite put into words.

Take another everyday example: typing on your phone. When auto-complete suggests the next word, it's making predictions just like your brain does when you're finishing someone else's sentence. You both might be right most of time, but try explaining exactly how you knew what word would come next. You can't, and neither can the AI – yet both systems work remarkably well.

Let's look at more examples. Watch a professional baseball player catch a fly ball. They're solving complex physics equations in real-time – calculating trajectories, adjusting for wind speed, compensating for spin. Except they're not, really. If you asked them to explain the mathematics, they couldn't. They just look up, start running, and somehow end up in exactly the right spot. This is similar to how self-driving cars work – they don't solve complex equations to stay in their lane or avoid obstacles. Instead, they develop an intuitive understanding through experience, just like human drivers do.

Consider how you understand language. Right now, you're effortlessly processing these words, understanding concepts, making connections. But can you explain the exact rules you're following? When someone says "Time flies like an arrow," you instantly know what it means. But try explaining to a computer why this same pattern doesn't work for "Fruit flies like a banana." ChatGPT and other AI language models face similar challenges – they can engage in surprisingly human-like conversations, but neither they nor their creators can fully explain how they understand context and meaning.

Think about how you navigate through your hometown. You instinctively know the fastest route to work, when to take detours, which shortcuts work best at what times. GPS systems like Google Maps do something similar, but with a twist. While they process vast amounts of real-time data, they sometimes make choices that look wrong on paper but work better in practice – just like your intuitive shortcuts. Both you and the AI have developed a kind of wisdom that goes beyond simple rule-following.

Let's connect the dots from our earlier observations:

- Pure logic falls apart in the real world because reality is too messy

- Most of our intelligent behaviors happen without our being able to explain them

- Even our amazing brains have built-in limits to what they can understand

- The most successful AI systems often work in ways their creators can't fully explain

- Both human and artificial intelligence seem to work best when they develop their own intuitions

These aren't separate problems – they're all pointing to the same surprising truth.

Social media algorithms face the same challenges we do when deciding what's interesting or important. Just as you quickly scroll through your friend's photos, stopping only on the ones that catch your eye, these systems make split-second decisions about what content to show you. Neither you nor the AI can fully explain why certain things grab attention while others don't – it's a complex dance of pattern recognition that works better when we don't try to reduce it to simple rules.

Think about a jazz musician improvising. If you asked them to stop mid-performance and explain exactly why they chose each note, they couldn't tell you. More importantly, if they tried to plan and rationalize every note, the music would lose its soul. We see this same principle in AI-generated music and art. When AI systems try to create art by following strict rules, the results feel mechanical. But when they're allowed to develop their own patterns and associations, like Midjourney or DALL-E, they can create surprisingly creative and emotional pieces.

Consider how YouTube's recommendation system works. Like a friend who knows your taste in music, it suggests videos based on patterns it's noticed in your viewing history. But just as your friend might struggle to explain exactly why they knew you'd love a particular song, the AI's decision-making process is more sophisticated than "people who watched X also liked Y." It's developing a kind of intuition, much like human recommendations do.

Watch a child learning to ride a bike. Give them a physics lecture about gyroscopic forces and center of gravity, and they'll just fall over. Let them learn through feeling and intuition, and soon they're zooming around the neighborhood. This is exactly why modern AI systems learn through experience rather than pre-programmed rules – some knowledge simply can't be reduced to explicit instructions. It's the same reason why robots learn to walk through trial and error rather than precise programming of each joint movement.

This shows up everywhere once you start looking:

- A chef knows exactly when to flip a steak by feel, not by following a rulebook

- Smart home systems learn your preferences without you explicitly programming them

- You instantly know if a sentence sounds "wrong" without consulting grammar rules

- AI spam filters catch malicious emails using patterns they've learned, not just rules

- An experienced firefighter develops a sixth sense for when a building is about to collapse

- Medical AI can spot diseases in x-rays sometimes before human doctors notice them

In each case, trying to break these abilities down into step-by-step instructions actually makes them worse, not better. Modern password systems work the same way – instead of following strict rules about special characters and numbers, they're starting to recognize secure passwords through learned patterns, just like humans intuitively sense when something feels secure.

Think of how you recognize emotions in someone's voice. You can instantly tell if someone is happy, angry, or sad just from their tone. Modern AI customer service systems do this too – they can detect frustration in a caller's voice and adjust their responses accordingly. Neither you nor the AI can explain exactly how you recognize these emotional patterns, but you both do it effectively.

This turns our traditional thinking upside down. We usually assume that if we can't explain something, we just need to study it more carefully. But with intelligence, both human and artificial, the opposite might be true. The very things that make it work – its ability to handle uncertainty, adapt to new situations, and operate in the messy real world – might require it to function in ways that can't be fully explained.

Think of it like this: a map can never capture every detail of the real world – if it did, it would be as big and complex as the world itself, making it useless as a map. In the same way, maybe any explanation of intelligence that captured every detail would be as complex as intelligence itself, making it no explanation at all.

This has huge implications for AI development. Instead of trying to create systems where every decision can be traced and explained, maybe we need to embrace systems that, like human intelligence, develop their own intuitions and patterns that work without being fully explainable. The most advanced AI systems today, like deep learning networks, already work this way – and they're the closest we've come to replicating human-like capabilities.

Consider how your smartphone's predictive text has gotten to know your writing style, or how your smart thermostat has learned your temperature preferences. These systems work best when they're allowed to develop their own understanding of your patterns, rather than following rigid, pre-programmed rules.

It's a beautiful irony: perhaps the key to understanding intelligence is accepting that some parts of it must remain beyond our understanding. Like trying to see your own eyes without a mirror, or trying to lift yourself up by your bootstraps, maybe there are some fundamental limits to how completely any intelligent system – human or artificial – can understand itself.

As we continue exploring intelligence, this insight offers a new perspective. Instead of seeing the unexplainable aspects of intelligence as problems to be solved, we might need to recognize them as essential features to be preserved. The path to creating true artificial intelligence might not lie in making everything logical and explainable, but in embracing and working with the inherently mysterious nature of intelligence itself. Just as we don't need to understand exactly how our brain works to use it effectively, maybe the future of AI lies in creating systems that can function brilliantly without us fully understanding how they do it.

Looking ahead

Imagine you're teaching a teenager to drive. You might start by giving them a rulebook: stop at red lights, maintain safe following distance, check mirrors regularly. But we all know that becoming a good driver involves much more than memorizing rules. It requires developing instincts, reading subtle cues from other drivers, and gaining a "feel" for the car that no manual can teach. This same pattern – the limitation of pure rules and the importance of learned intuition – mirrors the fascinating journey of artificial intelligence.

These insights about the mysterious nature of intelligence didn't come easily. Like many profound truths, they emerged only after decades of trying the opposite approach – attempting to build intelligence through pure logic and explicit rules. Just as early driving instructors might have thought they could create perfect drivers through detailed rulebooks, early AI researchers believed they could create thinking machines through pure logic.

Think about how you learned to cook. Maybe you started with precise recipes, measuring every ingredient exactly. But over time, you developed an intuition – a pinch of this, a dash of that, adjusting the heat just by looking at the pan. This evolution from rigid rules to fluid understanding perfectly captures the revolution that transformed our approach to artificial intelligence.

Our story begins in the 1950s, when brilliant mathematicians and computer scientists first dreamed of creating thinking machines. It was the dawn of the computer age – a time of unprecedented optimism. These pioneers had just witnessed the creation of machines that could perform calculations millions of times faster than humans. The next step seemed obvious: if computers could handle mathematics so well, surely they could handle any logical task. Armed with the newly invented computer and inspired by the apparent logic of human thought, they embarked on what they thought would be a straightforward journey.

The early AI researchers approached intelligence like engineers building a clock. Every gear, every movement, would be precisely specified and controlled. Their logic was compelling: human thinking seems to follow rules, computers are good at following rules, so building an intelligent machine should be just a matter of finding the right rules. It's similar to how we might initially think teaching a robot to walk just requires programming the right sequence of leg movements.

What happened next would challenge everything they thought they knew about the nature of intelligence and computation. Simple tasks that any child could do – like recognizing a cat in a photo or understanding a joke – proved incredibly difficult to reduce to logical rules. It was like trying to write down exact instructions for how to maintain your balance while riding a bicycle – the more detailed the instructions became, the less useful they were.

Their journey – and their discoveries – would lay the groundwork for modern artificial intelligence, while revealing fundamental truths about how intelligence really works. Today, we see the fruits of these lessons in every smartphone app that recognizes your face, every virtual assistant that understands your voice, and every recommendation system that seems to know what you'll like before you do. None of these modern AI systems relies on the kind of rigid logic those early pioneers imagined. Instead, they learn and adapt, much like a human brain.

Let's trace this fascinating history, not just to understand what happened, but to avoid repeating the same mistakes as we push toward new frontiers in artificial intelligence. The story of AI's evolution from logic to learning holds valuable lessons for everyone – from tech developers to everyday users of AI technology. It reminds us that sometimes the path to success involves embracing complexity and uncertainty rather than trying to eliminate them.

As we explore this journey, you'll see parallels to many aspects of human learning and development. From language acquisition to skill mastery, from artistic creativity to scientific discovery, the tension between rigid rules and flexible adaptation plays out again and again. Understanding this history helps us understand not just artificial intelligence, but human intelligence as well.

In the next section, we'll dive into the specific challenges these early AI pioneers faced, and how their "failures" ultimately led to breakthroughs that power the AI systems we use every day. Their story is more relevant than ever as we grapple with questions about the future of AI, human-machine collaboration, and the very nature of intelligence itself.

References & Sources

Chess Computer Milestone

Deep Blue Defeats Garry Kasparov in Chess Match
The New York Times, May 12, 1997
This historic match marked the first time a computer defeated
a reigning world champion under standard chess tournament
time controls.

Early AI Predictions

Machines Who Think
Pamela McCorduck
First published 1979, Updated 2004
Documents the optimistic predictions of early AI researchers,
including Herbert Simon's famous 1957 prediction about ma-
chines matching human capabilities.

Japanese Fifth Generation Project

*The Fifth Generation: Japan's Computer Challenge to
the World*
Edward Feigenbaum and Pamela McCorduck
Addison-Wesley, 1983
Chronicles Japan's ambitious AI project and its eventual out-
comes.

MIT Summer Vision Project

The Summer Vision Project
MIT AI Memo 100, July 1966
Original memo by Seymour Papert describing the proposed
summer project to solve computer vision.

Machine Translation Anecdote

"The whisky was invisible", or Persistent myths of MT

J Hutchins

MT News International, 1995

Traces early appearances of the "The whisky was invisible" / The vodka is good but the meat is rotten" anecdote.

DARPA Grand Challenge

Red Team Preparing for $1 Million Robotics Race Across the Desert

Carnegie Mellon News, March 13, 2004

Details the outcomes of the first DARPA Grand Challenge and why even advanced vehicles failed to complete the course.

Firefighter Decision Study

Sources of Power: How People Make Decisions

Gary Klein

MIT Press, 1998

Contains the original research on how fire ground commanders make rapid decisions under pressure.

XCON Expert System

R1: An Expert in the Computer Systems Domain

John McDermott

Proceedings of the First AAAI Conference on Artificial Intelligence, 1980

Details the development of XCON.

The Early Quest

History of AI approaches

Imagine you're in the 1950s. The first computers have just emerged - room-sized machines that can calculate faster than any human. Television was bringing the world into living rooms, the atomic age has dawned, jets are conquering the skies, and the impossible seems within reach. In this atmosphere of technological wonder, a group of brilliant scientists asked themselves: "If we can build machines that calculate, why not machines that think?"

These pioneers gathered at Dartmouth College in 1956 for what would become a historic meeting. Today, when we casually chat with digital assistants or watch robots perform complex tasks, their question might seem obvious. But in 1956, it was revolutionary - like asking if we could build a machine that could dream or fall in love.

They weren't just optimistic - they were absolutely convinced they were on the verge of cracking the code of human intelligence. Herbert Simon, a future Nobel laureate, confidently declared in 1957 that computers would match human intelligence within ten years. Marvin Minsky, a brilliant mathematician at MIT, assured the world that artificial intelligence would be solved within a generation. Looking back, it's easy to smile at their optimism -

but in their shoes, wouldn't we have felt the same? After all, they were witnessing technological miracles almost daily.

Their early successes seemed to confirm everything they believed. They created programs that could prove mathematical theorems faster than mathematicians - imagine a calculator that could not just solve equations, but discover new mathematical truths! They built chess-playing machines that improved year after year. When their programs solved complex logical puzzles in seconds, it felt like they had discovered the secret recipe for intelligence itself.

Money and talent poured in, much like today's tech startups attracting billions in investment. MIT, Stanford, and Carnegie Mellon established major AI laboratories. These weren't quiet academic corners - they were buzzing with energy and ambition, filled with young researchers convinced they were about to change the world. Corporate giants like IBM and Xerox opened their checkbooks wide. The Pentagon, seeing the military potential, funded ambitious projects through DARPA. Everyone wanted a piece of the future.

But here's where things get interesting. These pioneers focused on what they saw as the pinnacle of human thought: chess, mathematical proofs, logical puzzles. It would be like trying to understand human intelligence today by focusing solely on solving crossword puzzles.

They assumed that if they could master these "intellectual" challenges, everyday tasks like recognizing faces or catching a ball would be simple in comparison.

Think about this: we find it incredibly easy to recognize a friend's face in a crowd, even if they've changed their hairstyle or grown a beard. But try writing down the exact rules you use to do this. Not so easy, is it? The early AI researchers were essentially trying to write instruction manuals for things our brains do automatically.

Different groups took different approaches to the challenge. Some worked on natural language, trying to teach computers to understand human speech and writing. If you've ever wondered why it took so long to get from those early computers to something like modern translation tools, this helps explain why - language turned out to be far messier than anyone imagined. Others tackled computer vision, attempting to give machines the gift of sight. Still others focused on knowledge representation - trying to capture all of human knowledge in logical formulas.

But underneath all these efforts lay one fundamental assumption: that intelligence was essentially logical, that thinking could be reduced to explicit rules and formulas. It seemed so obvious that few questioned it. If you'd asked them how else intelligence might work, they might have looked at you as strangely as if you'd suggested computers should run on wishes instead of electricity.

This belief in logic and rules would dominate AI research for decades. It would produce impressive demonstrations and fuel periodic waves of excitement about breakthroughs just around the corner. But it would also lead to profound disappointments as researchers kept bumping into an uncomfortable reality: real intelligence seemed to involve something more than just following logical rules.

Think about how you catch a baseball. Are you solving physics equations in your head? Or consider how you know whether someone is joking or being serious. These seemingly simple tasks involve something more mysterious than logical rules - something these early researchers struggled to capture.

Their story isn't just history - it's a lesson about how our assumptions can both guide and limit us. They weren't wrong to pursue logical approaches; they were wrong in assuming it was the only way. Today's AI researchers have learned from this history, combining logical reasoning with learning from experience, much like humans do.

Looking back at these pioneers from our perspective - with AI assistants in our pockets and algorithms suggesting our next purchase - we might be tempted to smile at their optimism. But imagine what they would think of our world, where machines can recognize faces, understand speech, and even generate art. In many ways, we're living in the future they dreamed of, just not quite in the way they imagined it.

As we'll see, the path to true artificial intelligence would require embracing something these early researchers tried their best to eliminate: the beautiful uncertainty that makes intelligence possible. Their journey teaches us that sometimes the biggest breakthroughs come not from following our initial assumptions, but from being willing to question them when reality points us in a different direction.

The dream of perfectly logical systems

Imagine a mind that never makes mistakes. A mind free from bias, untouched by emotion, unclouded by uncertainty. A mind that reaches conclusions through pure, perfect logic. This wasn't just a scientific goal for early AI researchers – it was the culmination of a philosophical dream that had captivated thinkers for centuries.

The story begins in the Age of Reason, when philosophers believed that pure logic could unlock all of life's mysteries. René Descartes, the French philosopher who gave us "I think, therefore I am," imagined that all human knowledge could be built from simple, logical steps – like a massive mathematical proof. Gottfried Leibniz took this even further. Troubled by endless human disagreements, he envisioned a universal logical language that could settle any dispute through calculation. "Let us calculate," he declared, believing that even our deepest moral and philosophical questions could be resolved through pure logic.

These weren't just abstract ideas gathering dust in philosophy books. When the first AI researchers began their work in the 1950s, they saw themselves as finally fulfilling this centuries-old dream. They were the inheritors of rationalism – the philosophical tradition that placed pure reason above all else. Just as Descartes had tried to build all knowledge from logical foundations, they would build minds from logical rules.

The logic of their approach seemed irrefutable. After all, computers themselves were triumphs of logical design – every operation, from simple addition to complex calculations, reduced to the manipulation of ones and zeros according to precise rules. If human intelligence was fundamentally logical (and why wouldn't it be?), then computers should be the perfect vessel for creating artificial minds.

Consider SHRDLU, a program created at MIT in the early 1970s. It operated in a simple world of colored blocks, where it could answer questions and follow commands about stacking and arranging them. SHRDLU seemed to understand English perfectly within its tiny domain. Ask it to "pick up the big red block" and it would do so flawlessly, even refusing impossible commands with logical explanations. It was like having a perfectly logical child who never misunderstood instructions – as long as you only talked about blocks.

Or take MYCIN, developed at Stanford to diagnose blood infections. Instead of trying to replicate the intuitive way doctors think, its creators interviewed medical experts and turned their knowledge into hundreds of precise if-then rules. If the patient has symptom X and test result Y, then conclude Z with certainty percentage P. It was like trying to turn the art of medicine into pure mathematics.

Think of how they imagined an ideal intelligent system would work: Start with basic facts and rules. Apply logic step by step. Never guess. Never use hunches. Never make a move without complete logical justification. It would be like Mr. Spock from Star Trek, but without even the occasional raised eyebrow.

There was something almost poetic about this vision. Many researchers spoke about their work with an almost religious reverence. They weren't just writing computer programs – they were creating pure reason itself, freed from the messy biological constraints of human brains. It was an intoxicating dream that connected them to centuries of philosophical thought about the power of logic.

This quest for perfect logic shaped everything they did. When they tackled language understanding, they didn't study how humans actually communicate – with all our subtle hints, unspoken assumptions, and contextual understanding. Instead, they tried to create rigid logical rules for breaking down sentences. They built programs like STUDENT, which could solve algebra word problems by turning them into equations, but was baffled by simple phrases that any child would understand.

Their approach to problem-solving was similarly rigid. Rather than notice how humans actually solve problems – often through intuition, trial and error, and those mysterious "Aha!" moments – they built systems that methodically examined every possible solution like a chess computer calculating moves. The General Problem Solver (GPS), another pioneering program, could solve perfectly defined puzzles but was helpless when faced with the kind of fuzzy, open-ended challenges we handle every day.

Even their view of learning was shaped by this dream of perfect logic. Instead of studying how humans learn – through experience, imitation, and plenty of mistakes – they tried to create systems that would learn only through formal logical deduction. Imagine trying to learn to ride a bicycle by deriving it from Newton's laws of motion!

But perhaps most importantly, this dream changed how they thought about intelligence itself. Rather than seeing intelligence as the messy, adaptable thing we observe in nature, they redefined it as perfect logical reasoning. It's as if they looked at a bird flying and concluded that the essence of flight was solving differential equations.

The dream was beautiful. It was elegant. It promised not just to match human intelligence but to perfect it. Following in the footsteps of Descartes and Leibniz, these researchers believed they were finally building the perfect logical minds that philosophers had only imagined. There was just one small problem: reality had other plans.

Looking back now, we can see how this dream of perfect logic both drove the field forward and led it astray. The desire for logical perfection gave researchers clear goals and produced impressive demonstrations. But it also blinded them to something crucial about how intelligence actually works – something that has more to do with adaptation and uncertainty than with perfect logical rules.

As we'll see next, this pursuit of perfect logic would lead AI into some fascinating dead ends. But sometimes we learn more from our elegant failures than from our messy successes.

Rule-based systems and their limitations

Picture yourself walking into a research lab in 1975. The air buzzes with excitement as researchers huddle around bulky computer terminals. They're not just programming – they're teaching computers to think like experts. "We've cracked it," they'd tell you with gleaming eyes. "We've figured out how to capture human expertise in computer code!" This wasn't just tech enthusiasm – it was a revolution in how we thought about artificial intelligence.

The idea seemed beautifully simple: human experts use logical rules to make decisions, right? A doctor thinks "if fever AND sore throat, then consider strep." A geologist reasons "if we find this mineral formation, check for gold deposits nearby." So why not just interview experts, write down their rules, and give them to a computer? It was like trying to create a digital apprentice that could learn from the masters.

The star of this era was MYCIN, a medical diagnosis system developed at Stanford that became the poster child for what these systems could achieve. Imagine a digital doctor that interviewed patients through a computer terminal. "Is your fever above 101°F?" it would ask. "What do the bacteria in your blood look like?" Each answer would trigger new questions, following chains of reasoning that could rival an experienced physician's thought process.

MYCIN wasn't just guessing – it was using over 600 carefully crafted rules, each with its own certainty factor. "If the infection is in the blood AND the bacteria are rod-shaped AND gram-negative, THEN there's a 70% chance it's E. coli." When tested against human doctors, MYCIN didn't just hold its own – it sometimes outperformed them. In one study, it matched or exceeded the accuracy of infectious disease specialists. Remember, this was the 1970s, when most people still thought computers were just fancy calculators.

The success stories kept rolling in. XCON, developed for Digital Equipment Corporation, was like having a genius computer engineer in a box. Configuring a computer system back then wasn't like adding items to your Amazon cart – it was a complex puzzle of ensuring thousands of components would work together. XCON knew over 10,000 rules about which parts could connect to what, how much power they needed, and how they should be arranged. It saved the company millions by catching compatibility issues that even expert engineers missed.

Then there was PROSPECTOR, the digital geologist. Think of it as CSI for mineral deposits. It would analyze geological data using rules that mimicked expert reasoning: "If we see these types of rocks AND these chemical traces, THEN there's likely a deposit nearby." Skeptics scoffed – until PROSPECTOR discovered a molybdenum deposit worth $100 million in Washington state that human experts had overlooked. Suddenly, everyone wanted their own AI prospector.

DENDRAL showed how these systems could revolutionize scientific research. Chemists usually spent hours or days analyzing mass spectrometry data to figure out molecular structures. DENDRAL could do it in minutes by applying expert rules about chemical bonds and molecular patterns. It was like having a tireless lab assistant with perfect memory and lightning-fast analytical skills.

Corporate America saw these successes and went all in. A new profession emerged – "knowledge engineers" who specialized in interviewing experts and translating their wisdom into computer rules. Major companies set up AI divisions. Investment bankers dreamed of automated financial advisors. Insurance companies imagined automated underwriters. Even lawyers thought they could encode legal expertise into rules.

Japan launched its ambitious Fifth Generation Computer Project, aiming to leapfrog America in AI technology. They planned to build computers that could reason using massive databases of rules, understand natural language, and even engage in conversation. The project would eventually spend billions. The future seemed clear: soon we'd have digital experts in every field.

But then reality started throwing curveballs, and they came from unexpected directions.

The first problem emerged during the knowledge engineering process itself. Imagine trying to interview a master chef about how they cook. "How do you know when the pasta is done?" you ask. "I just know by looking at it," they say. "But what exactly do you look for?" "Well... it's hard to explain... you develop a feel for it." This wasn't just about cooking – the same pattern emerged everywhere.

Expert radiologists could spot tumors in x-rays with amazing accuracy but struggled to explain exactly how they knew what to look for. Master mechanics could diagnose engine problems by sound but couldn't translate that knowledge into precise rules. It turned out that much of human expertise isn't in conscious rules at all – it's in patterns and intuitions built up through years of experience.

Even when experts could articulate rules, the resulting systems had a peculiar weakness: they were brittle. They worked perfectly on textbook cases but fell apart in unusual situations. MYCIN might excel at diagnosing common infections but be completely stumped by an unusual case that didn't fit its rules. It was like having a GPS that works flawlessly until you hit a road construction detour – exactly when you need it most.

Maintaining these systems turned into a nightmare. XCON's initial success led DEC to keep expanding it, eventually reaching over 50,000 rules. But as the rules multiplied, the system became increasingly unpredictable. Adding new rules was like playing high-stakes Jenga – each addition risked toppling the whole structure. What started as clean, logical systems became tangled webs of special cases and exceptions.

Imagine trying to write down every rule for riding a bicycle. Start with the basics: "If leaning right, turn handlebars right to balance." Simple enough. But then you need exceptions: "Unless you're moving very slowly." "Unless you're on loose gravel." "Unless there's a strong crosswind." "Unless you're carrying an awkward package." The list never ends. Human cyclists handle all these situations effortlessly, but trying to capture that knowledge in rules was like trying to empty the ocean with a teaspoon.

But the deepest problem was something scientists called the "frame problem" – determining what's relevant to a decision. This sounds abstract until you try to program a computer to handle everyday situations. Consider a simple task: getting coffee from your kitchen. You automatically know to check if you have coffee, if the machine is working, if you have time before your next meeting. You don't waste time checking if your neighbor's dog is asleep, or what the weather is like in

Paris, or whether Neptune is aligned with Mars.

How do you know what to ignore? There's no logical way to list all the things that might matter and all the things that definitely don't. The frame problem shows up everywhere. When you're driving and hear a siren, you instantly know to consider its direction, what kind of emergency vehicle it might be, and how to get out of its way. You don't waste mental energy wondering if the siren relates to your breakfast choices or weekend plans.

Or take something medical systems like MYCIN had to handle: diagnosing chest pain. Should the system consider the patient's age? Obviously. Their diet? Probably. Their job? Maybe – stress matters. The color of their shirt? Probably not. Whether they own a cat? Actually, that could matter – it might be an allergy. Whether they've traveled recently? Yes – what if it's a tropical disease? Whether they like jazz music? Probably not, but what if... The list of potentially relevant factors is endless.

The frame problem revealed something profound about human intelligence. We don't just follow rules – we understand context. We have common sense. We know what's relevant and what isn't, not through logical deduction, but through some deeper understanding of how the world works.

By the late 1980s, the limitations were clear. Rule-based systems worked well in narrow, well-defined domains – like playing chess or calculating tax deductions. But they failed at the kind of flexible, intuitive reasoning that humans do naturally. You could build a system that played perfect chess, but not one that could explain why chess is fun or adapt its strategy when playing against a child.

The dream of capturing human expertise in logical rules had hit a wall. But this failure would teach us something profound about the nature of intelligence itself. Human thinking isn't just about following rules – it's about understanding context, managing relevance, and drawing on deep background knowledge in ways we're still trying to comprehend.

The rule-based systems era left us with valuable lessons. It showed that some types of expertise can be captured in rules, but also revealed the limits of purely logical approaches to AI. Perhaps most importantly, it forced us to think harder about what makes human intelligence special. Sometimes our most elegant theories fail because reality is messier – and more interesting – than we imagined.

What we learned from this "failure" would eventually lead AI research in exciting new directions, pushing us to develop more sophisticated approaches to artificial intelligence that could better handle the complexity and nuance of human-like reasoning. These new directions would fundamentally reshape our understanding of both artificial and human intelligence.

Why early speech/handwriting recognition failed

Imagine trying to teach someone to understand speech by giving them a rulebook. "When you hear this sound, it's an 'A.' When you hear that sound, it's a 'B.' When these sounds come in this order, it's a word." Sounds absurd, right? Yet this was exactly how early AI researchers approached speech recognition in the 1950s and 60s.

The logic seemed impeccable. After all, language has rules. We learn these rules in school – phonics, grammar, sentence structure. Handwriting too follows patterns – every "A" is basically two diagonal lines meeting at the top with a crossbar. Just turn these rules into computer code, and voila! Except it wasn't that simple. Not even close.

The technical approach these early systems used was called "template matching." For speech recognition, researchers would record someone saying each sound, create a template of what that sound's waveform looked like, then try to match new speech against these templates. For handwriting, they'd create idealized templates of each letter and try to match input against these patterns.

The problems with this approach became apparent almost immediately. Speech waveforms for the same word look dramatically different when spoken by different people, or even by the same person at different times. A template of someone saying "hello" might show five distinct sound peaks – but speak it faster or slower, with different emphasis, or with any emotion, and those peaks blur, stretch, merge, or disappear entirely.

The first speech recognition systems were almost comically limited. They might work if you spoke... like... this... in... a... quiet... room. But try natural conversation? Add a little background noise? Speak with an accent? The systems fell apart completely. Imagine a GPS that only works if you drive exactly 30 mph on a perfectly straight road on a sunny day – not very useful in the real world.

The technical limitations were severe. Background noise would create false peaks in the audio signal. Different microphones would capture different frequency ranges. Room acoustics would add echoes and reverberations. Even slight variations in distance from the microphone would change the signal strength. The templates simply couldn't handle this vast range of real-world variations.

Handwriting recognition faced similar problems. The systems could maybe handle text that looked like it came from a first-grade penmanship workbook. But real handwriting? The messy, rushed notes you scribble during a phone call? The quick signature on a credit card receipt? Not a chance.

The template-matching approach to handwriting was particularly brittle. Letters in real handwriting often connect to each other, making it impossible to isolate individual characters. People frequently combine or overlap strokes in ways that break the idealized templates. Something as simple as writing at a slight angle would throw off the entire recognition process.

The deeper researchers dug, the more they realized how naive their initial assumptions had been. Think about how you speak differently when you're excited, or tired, or talking to a child, or giving a presentation. Think about how your handwriting changes when you're in a hurry, or using a different pen, or writing on an uneven surface. These aren't just minor variations – they're fundamental to how human communication works.

Here's a simple experiment: try saying the word "okay" in different ways – as a question, as agreement, as skepticism, as excitement. Same word, completely different meanings. The waveforms for these variations would look entirely different. The pitch might rise at the end for a question, or drop for skepticism. The duration might stretch for emphasis or compress for quick agreement. Now imagine trying to write rules for a computer to understand all these variations. Or try writing your signature five times – they'll all be slightly different, yet instantly recognizable to a human. How do you write rules for that?

The failures were most revealing when it came to ambiguity. Consider this sentence: "Time flies like an arrow." Simple, right? But a computer trying to parse this with logical rules faces a nightmare. Is "time" a noun or a verb? Are we talking about measuring flying insects? Who exactly is liking this arrow? Humans resolve these ambiguities effortlessly using context and common sense – qualities that proved impossible to reduce to logical rules.

Or take the classic example of reading graffiti. Humans can usually read even heavily stylized graffiti text, but rule-based systems were completely stumped. They couldn't handle text where the letters overlapped, or had unusual decorations, or broke basic rules of letter formation. Yet these "rule violations" are exactly what gives graffiti its artistic appeal.

These failures pointed to a deeper problem with early AI's entire approach. The researchers had assumed that human abilities could be reduced to logical rules and templates. But human speech recognition doesn't work by matching sounds to templates – it's a sophisticated process that integrates acoustic information with linguistic knowledge, context, and understanding of the speaker's intent. Similarly, human reading doesn't work by matching letter shapes – it's a complex process that combines visual perception with language understanding and real-world knowledge.

By the mid-1980s, speech and handwriting recognition had become cautionary tales in AI – examples of how not to approach the problem of artificial intelligence. The failures revealed something profound: human intelligence isn't about following rules or matching templates. It's about something far more subtle and complex.

These early failures also contained important clues about the true nature of intelligence. When humans understand speech or read handwriting, we're not following rules or matching templates – we're pattern matching at multiple levels simultaneously, using context, drawing on vast experience, and integrating multiple types of information. We don't just process the sound or visual input – we understand the meaning behind it.

This realization would eventually lead AI research in a completely different direction. Instead of trying to explicitly program rules and templates, researchers would begin exploring approaches that could learn patterns from data, handle uncertainty and variation, and integrate multiple types of information. The problem wasn't just that early systems weren't sophisticated enough – it was that the entire approach of trying to reduce human abilities to logical rules and templates was fundamentally flawed.

The lesson was clear: to create truly intelligent systems, we needed to better understand how human intelligence actually works, not how we imagine it works. This insight would prove crucial as AI entered its next phase, moving away from rigid rules and templates toward more flexible, learning-based approaches.

The explainability trap

Imagine asking a professional cyclist how they stay balanced on their bike. They might talk about keeping their weight centered, watching their speed, and turning the handlebars to correct tilts. Now imagine trying to build a robot based on those instructions. It would fall over instantly. Yet small children learn to ride bikes without understanding any of these principles. This paradox – where the explainable is hard to automate and the automatic is hard to explain – lies at the heart of AI's early struggles.

I call this the "explainability trap," and it turned many AI projects inside out. The trap works in both directions: skills that humans can explain clearly often prove surprisingly difficult to automate, while skills that computers master easily often resist human explanation. This misalignment between explanation and automation challenged fundamental assumptions about artificial intelligence.

Take chess. Grandmasters can fill books with strategic principles: control the center, protect your king, develop your pieces. Early AI researchers dutifully turned these insights into computer code, expecting to capture the essence of chess mastery. But today's chess engines, which can defeat any human, don't play anything like this. They evaluate millions of positions through methods that look nothing like human strategic thinking. The human-explainable principles of chess strategy turned out to be less useful than brute-force calculation and pattern matching.

Or consider a radiologist reading an X-ray. Ask them how they spot a tumor, and they'll describe a careful, systematic process of checking specific areas and looking for certain characteristics. But track their eye movements, and you'll find they often zero in on abnormalities almost instantly, before any conscious analysis. Their explicit procedure isn't actually how they make their best diagnoses – it's just their best attempt to explain an intuitive process.

The trap becomes even clearer in physical skills. A professional tennis player can explain proper serving technique in great detail – grip position, ball toss, weight transfer, follow-through. Yet a robot programmed with these instructions would serve terribly. Meanwhile, the unconscious adjustments the player makes for wind, fatigue, or court position – things they might not even realize they're doing – prove crucial to their success.

This disconnect appears everywhere. Ask an expert baker how they know when dough has been kneaded enough, and they might talk about elasticity and gluten development. But in practice, they rely on subtle tactile feedback that's almost impossible to verbalize. Try to program a robot with their verbal instructions, and you'll get inconsistent results. The real expertise lies in patterns they've internalized through experience, not in their conscious explanations.

The explainability trap created a fascinating bias in AI research. The more clearly humans could explain a skill, the more researchers rushed to encode those explanations into software. Think of it like trying to teach someone to catch a ball by giving them equations for projectile motion. The physics is perfectly accurate, but it's not how humans actually catch balls. We use unconscious processes that incorporate countless variables – the ball's spin, air resistance, our own movement – without explicit calculation.

This trap became especially evident in language. We can all explain basic grammar rules: nouns, verbs, subject-verb agreement. Early AI researchers built elaborate systems based on these rules. But try explaining to someone how you know that "I'm feeling blue" means sad rather than literally turning blue, or how you know whether "Time flies like an arrow" is about fast time or arrow-loving insects. These subtle aspects of language understanding resist explicit explanation, yet humans grasp them effortlessly.

The pursuit of logical, explainable systems led researchers down numerous dead ends. They built programs that could solve algebra problems by following the same steps taught in schools, only to find that mathematical reasoning involves much more than explicit rule-following. They created systems that could parse sentences according to grammatical rules, only to discover that language comprehension requires vast amounts of world knowledge that resists formal representation.

Even seemingly straightforward tasks revealed this pattern. Consider face recognition. Humans can easily explain what makes a face recognizable – two eyes, a nose, a mouth in the right positions. Early researchers created systems that looked for these features. But these systems failed miserably at actual face recognition, while modern systems that use less explainable pattern-matching approaches work remarkably well.

What makes this trap so sneaky is that it plays into our natural bias about intelligence. We tend to think our conscious, verbal explanations accurately describe how our minds work. But that's like thinking we understand how our digestive system works just because we can explain what we like to eat. Most of our intelligence operates below the surface of consciousness, in ways we can't directly access or explain.

The trap also reinforced AI's early focus on logic and explicit reasoning. If a skill could be explained logically, researchers assumed it could be automated through logical rules. This led them to concentrate on tasks that seemed amenable to logical decomposition, like mathematical theorem proving or game playing with clear rules. Meanwhile, they struggled with tasks that humans perform effortlessly but can't explain logically, like understanding speech or recognizing objects.

Breaking free from this trap required a radical shift in thinking. Instead of trying to program computers with human-provided explanations of intelligence, researchers began exploring approaches that could learn from experience – even if they couldn't explain their decisions in human terms. It's like the difference between trying to write down rules for recognizing cats versus showing a system millions of cat pictures and letting it figure out the patterns for itself.

This insight extends far beyond AI. It suggests that human self-knowledge has serious limits. The stories we tell ourselves about how we think might be more like a news anchor confidently explaining the day's events rather than a security camera faithfully recording them. We're great at creating plausible explanations for our actions, but these explanations might have little to do with our actual cognitive processes.

Consider expertise in any field. Experts often develop intuitions they can't fully explain – the doctor who "just knows" something's wrong, the mechanic who can diagnose an engine by its sound, the artist who instinctively knows when a composition works. Their verbal explanations of these abilities tend to be incomplete or even misleading. The real expertise lies in pattern recognition abilities built through experience, not in explicit rules or principles.

True intelligence, it turns out, might be less about following explicit rules and more about pattern recognition, intuition, and learning from experience – precisely the capabilities that resist reduction to clear explanations. It's a humbling realization: perhaps we're not as transparent to ourselves as we'd like to believe.

As one AI researcher put it: "We thought we were building a system to think like humans. Instead, we learned that we don't really know how humans think." This insight would prove crucial as AI entered its next phase, moving away from rule-based systems toward approaches that could learn and adapt on their own. The future of AI would lie not in capturing human explanations, but in developing systems that could learn patterns and relationships in ways that might not be humanly explainable at all.

Turning point: from rules to randomness

The story of early AI contains both cautionary tales and valuable lessons. The logical, rule-based approaches failed not because they were wrong, but because they were incomplete. They captured the surface-level explanations of intelligence while missing the deeper, harder-to-articulate processes that drive human cognition. The explainability trap led researchers down appealing but ultimately unproductive paths.

The failures of early AI revealed something profound about the nature of intelligence itself. Human cognition, it turned out, wasn't a collection of neat logical rules but rather a complex interplay of conscious reasoning and unconscious pattern recognition. Our ability to recognize faces, understand language, or catch a ball didn't stem from following explicit rules – it emerged from processes that were far more fluid and adaptable.

Even in domains where rules seemed most applicable, like chess or mathematical problem-solving, the most effective approaches turned out to be quite different from human-style strategic thinking. The chess engines that eventually beat grandmasters didn't win by better understanding classical chess principles – they won by evaluating vast numbers of possibilities in ways that bore little resemblance to human thought.

Yet these failures were productive in their own way. They revealed crucial insights about the nature of intelligence – insights that would prove vital as AI entered its next phase. The limitations of rule-based systems pushed researchers to question their fundamental assumptions about what intelligence is and how it emerges. Perhaps most importantly, they showed that building intelligent machines would require understanding not just logic and rules, but the messier, less predictable aspects of natural intelligence.

This realization prompted researchers to look more closely at how nature itself solves complex problems. How does evolution produce intricate adaptations without any central planning? How do brains learn and adapt without explicit programming? How do complex systems like weather patterns or ecosystems maintain themselves without following rigid rules?

The answer, surprisingly, involved an element that early AI researchers had largely treated as an enemy to be eliminated: randomness. In nature, randomness isn't a bug – it's a feature. Random mutations drive evolution. Random neural firing patterns help brains learn. Random fluctuations allow systems to explore new possibilities and avoid getting stuck in rigid patterns.

The shift from rigid rules to embracing uncertainty would mark a fundamental turning point in AI's development. Instead of trying to program computers with perfect logical rules, researchers began exploring approaches that could learn from experience, adapt to new situations, and handle uncertainty. This meant moving away from brittle, deterministic systems toward more flexible, probabilistic approaches that could deal with the messiness of the real world.

This new direction would lead AI research into previously unexplored territory. How could randomness be harnessed constructively rather than just treated as noise to be eliminated? How could systems learn from incomplete or uncertain information? How could artificial intelligence handle the kind of ambiguity and flexibility that comes so naturally to biological intelligence?

As we'll see in the next chapter, nature has a surprising secret ingredient that early AI researchers largely ignored: randomness. Far from being a flaw to eliminate, this controlled chaos turns out to be essential to how natural systems – from evolution to brains to weather patterns – create complex, adaptive behavior. Understanding how nature uses randomness as a creative force would open up entirely new approaches to artificial intelligence, leading to breakthroughs that the early rule-based pioneers could hardly have imagined.

The shift from rules to randomness wouldn't just change how we build AI systems – it would transform our understanding of intelligence itself. The next chapter will explore how nature harnesses chaos to create order, and what this teaches us about building truly intelligent machines.

References & Sources

Early AI Logic Systems

The Quest for Artificial Intelligence: A History of Ideas and Achievements

Nils J. Nilsson

Cambridge University Press, 2009

Documents early AI researchers' focus on logic-based approaches and their underlying assumptions about machine intelligence.

Early Speech Recognition

Automatic Speech Recognition – A Brief History of the Technology Development

B.H. Juang and Lawrence R. Rabiner

Punlished 2005

Chronicles early attempts at speech recognition and the technical limitations that led to initial failures.

Explainable AI History

Interpretable Machine Learning: A Guide for Making Black Box Models Explainable

Christoph Molnar

Published 2019

Provides historical context for the evolution of explainable AI systems and their limitations.

AI Paradigm Shift

Deep Learning Revolution: Artificial Intelligence Meets Human Intelligence

Terrence J. Sejnowski

MIT Press, 2018

Describes the transition from rule-based systems to probabilistic approaches in AI development.

Nature's Secret Sauce

Randomness in nature

If you were tasked with designing a perfect system, you'd probably try to make it as precise and predictable as possible. That's exactly what early AI researchers did – and it's exactly where they went wrong. Nature, the greatest designer of all time, does something that seems completely counterintuitive: it embraces randomness.

Imagine walking through a forest. From a distance, it might look perfectly organized, like nature's version of a well-planned garden. But get closer, and you'll discover a beautiful chaos at work. Each tree trunk twists uniquely toward the light, branches spread in seemingly haphazard patterns. Dead trees create random gaps in the canopy where sunlight streams through, triggering an explosion of diverse plant life below. Moss creeps up bark in irregular patches, creating micro-ecosystems for countless tiny organisms. Even the forest floor, carpeted with leaves that fell in random patterns, creates unique pockets where seeds can germinate and new life can emerge.

This apparent disorder isn't just beautiful – it's crucial for survival. When a disease sweeps through, it might kill trees with certain genetic patterns, but the random variations ensure some will survive. When a storm hits, the irregular spacing of trees helps distribute the force of the wind. If one species struggles, another randomly positioned nearby might thrive in its place. Nature's messiness is its insurance policy.

The contrast with early AI systems is striking. Those first artificial brains were built like perfectly ordered gardens – every "neuron" connected in carefully planned patterns, every response predetermined, every output predictable. They were beautiful in their precision but collapsed at the slightest deviation from their expected input. Just as a perfectly symmetrical garden would be devastated by one storm, these early AIs couldn't handle the messy reality of the real world.

Look closer at any natural system, and you'll find this creative chaos at work. Watch a flock of birds respond to a predator – their escape patterns aren't pre-programmed but emerge from countless random adjustments. Observe how a river finds its path, not through careful planning but through countless random interactions between water, gravity, and terrain. Even your own thoughts aren't marching in straight lines – they're emerging from billions of neurons firing in patterns that incorporate random variation.

Think about how you learned to walk. You didn't solve differential equations to calculate the perfect angle for each joint. Instead, you wobbled, fell, adjusted randomly, and gradually found patterns that worked. Your brain didn't just execute a program – it explored possibilities through controlled randomness. Early AI researchers would have tried to program the perfect walk. Nature's approach? Try random variations and keep what works.

But – and this is the crucial part – nature isn't just throwing dice randomly. It's more like a master chef who knows exactly when to add a pinch of chaos to the recipe. I call this "controlled chaos." Evolution generates random mutations but selects them based on survival value. Your immune system creates random antibody variations but amplifies only those that work. Your brain's learning processes incorporate random noise but strengthen only the useful connections.

This insight would eventually revolutionize AI development. Modern AI systems succeed precisely because they've learned to embrace this controlled chaos. Neural networks introduce random variations during training. Reinforcement learning algorithms explicitly balance random exploration with focused exploitation. Language models include elements of randomness in their text generation to avoid getting stuck in repetitive patterns.

The lesson is clear: if we want to build truly intelligent systems, we need to stop fighting randomness and start harnessing it. Nature has been running this experiment for billions of years, and the results are in: randomness, properly controlled, isn't a force of destruction – it's a powerful tool for creation. Just as a forest's resilience comes from its beautiful chaos, our artificial intelligence needs to embrace the creative power of uncertainty.

Evolution and random mutations

Imagine you're playing a video game where you need to build the perfect racing car. Instead of designing it all at once, the game gives you a twist: you start with basic cars that have random features, race them, keep the best performers, mix their features, and add some random changes. At first, it seems like a strange way to design a car. But after many rounds, you end up with cars that are surprisingly effective – perhaps even better than what you might have designed from scratch.

This game-like process mirrors something fascinating we see in nature: evolution through random mutations and natural selection. It's like nature's own research and development department, but with an unusual approach – it tries countless random experiments and lets real-world results decide what works. What's even more fascinating is how modern AI has taken this idea and supercharged it.

Let me show you how this works in practice. When AI researchers develop what we call genetic algorithms, they're essentially running evolution on fast forward. Take that racing car example – a real genetic algorithm might represent each car as a string of digital "DNA" that encodes everything from wheel size to engine power. Just as biological DNA occasionally has random mutations, the algorithm introduces random changes to this code.

But here's where it gets clever. Just as nature doesn't just randomly mutate things and hope for the best, these algorithms use several evolution-inspired tricks:

- Crossover: Taking successful designs and mixing their features, like two parent cars producing offspring with traits from both

- Mutation: Adding random tweaks to keep exploring new possibilities

- Selection pressure: Only the best performers get to pass their traits to the next generation

- Population diversity: Maintaining a variety of different solutions to avoid getting stuck in dead ends

Back in the 1990s, computer scientist Karl Sims showed just how powerful this approach could be. His virtual creatures, evolving in a simulated ocean, developed swimming motions that no human designer had imagined. Some undulated like eels, others developed paddle-like appendages, and some found entirely novel ways to move through water. The key wasn't clever programming – it was letting random variations and selection do the creative work.

Today, this evolutionary approach has spread far beyond simple simulations. Modern AI systems use evolution-inspired techniques to solve incredibly complex problems:

- Antenna designers use genetic algorithms to create bizarre-looking but highly effective satellite antennas

- Neural network architects use evolutionary strategies to discover better network structures

- Roboticists use "evolutionary robotics" to develop better walking gaits and control systems

- Trading algorithms evolve their strategies by testing random variations in simulated markets

Think of it as nature's version of brainstorming on steroids. But instead of a room full of people throwing out ideas, you have millions of digital variations being tested simultaneously. Most fail – just like most mutations in nature – but the successful ones are preserved and built upon.

This approach has even influenced how we train the largest AI models. While systems like GPT don't literally use genetic algorithms, they employ similar principles of controlled randomness during training. During each training step, random noise helps these models explore different possibilities for how to process information, with successful patterns being reinforced over time.

Take Deep Mind's AlphaGo as another example. While it didn't use genetic algorithms directly, it embraced the same core principle: explore through randomness, learn from success. During training, it played millions of games against itself, trying random variations of moves and strategies. The successful patterns were reinforced, while failed approaches were discarded – just like natural selection, but at digital speed.

The power of this approach lies in its ability to find solutions that human designers might never imagine. Just as evolution produced the incredible diversity of life on Earth through countless random experiments, evolutionary algorithms can discover unexpected solutions to complex problems. They can explore vast possibility spaces that human designers could never fully investigate.

Modern AI success stories often involve this dance between randomness and selection. Whether it's language models finding new ways to combine words, trading algorithms discovering novel strategies, or robot controls learning efficient movements, controlled randomness helps these systems innovate and adapt. It's a beautiful example of how understanding nature's methods can help us build better artificial intelligence.

Who would have thought that random changes, properly filtered, could be such a powerful force for innovation? Nature figured this out billions of years ago. We're just beginning to apply these lessons to artificial intelligence, and the results are already remarkable. It's another reminder that sometimes the best way forward isn't to design the perfect solution, but to create conditions where good solutions can emerge through exploration and testing.

Brain's neural noise

Picture yourself trying to hold a full cup of coffee perfectly still. Impossible, right? Your hand makes tiny, random movements no matter how hard you try to keep it steady. For years, scientists thought this was just a flaw in our biological machinery – like static on an old radio that we just had to live with. But they were in for a surprise that would change how we think about both brains and AI.

Your brain is like a jazz club on a busy night – there's always some noise in the background. Every time your brain cells communicate, there's a bit of random static in their signals. But here's the mind-bending part: your brain actually needs this noise to work properly. It's like salt in cooking – the right amount makes everything work better. And when it comes to creativity, this noise might be the secret sauce we've been looking for.

Let's explore how this works in your brain during creative problem-solving. Imagine you're trying to come up with a new recipe using leftover ingredients. Your brain doesn't methodically check every possible combination like a computer might. Instead, it enters a state where neural noise helps it jump between different possibilities in unpredictable ways. One moment you're thinking about combining pasta with vegetables, then a random neural firing pattern makes you think of turning those same ingredients into a soup, and suddenly – thanks to another random connection – you remember a similar dish from your travels that could work perfectly.

This neural noise is crucial for creativity in countless ways. When you're stuck in a mental rut, random neural firing can help you break free by activating unexpected pathways in your brain. It allows you to discover unlikely connections that often lead to those "aha!" moments. The noise keeps your thinking flexible, preventing you from getting trapped in rigid patterns. Perhaps most importantly, it helps you see familiar things in new ways by adding variability to your perceptions.

Even your basic sensory processing uses this principle. Those tiny random movements in your hand holding the coffee cup? They're not a design flaw. They're part of your brain's active sensing system. By adding small random movements, your brain actually gathers more information about the cup's weight, position, and the liquid inside. It's like constantly taking slightly different snapshots of the same scene to build a richer understanding.

This insight is revolutionizing how we think about artificial intelligence. Modern AI systems are beginning to incorporate similar principles of creative noise. When generating text, language models now use controlled randomness to avoid getting stuck in repetitive patterns and to enable more creative writing. Neural networks have found ways to randomly shake things up during training, helping them learn more flexible and robust patterns. AI systems for creative tasks often include ways to adjust their "randomness level," just like a chef adjusting the amount of spice in a dish.

Take an AI system generating art, for instance. Without any randomness, it might get stuck producing variations of the same image. But add some controlled noise – similar to your brain's neural noise – and it can explore new artistic possibilities while still maintaining coherence. It's like giving the AI permission to "think outside the box" in a way that mirrors human creativity.

Even in more practical applications, this principle proves valuable. When an AI system is trying to optimize a complex process – like finding the best way to schedule deliveries or design a new product – adding controlled noise helps it escape dead ends and find better solutions. Just as your brain uses noise to avoid getting stuck in mental ruts, AI systems use randomness to avoid getting trapped in suboptimal solutions.

The implications go even deeper when we think about learning and memory. Your brain doesn't store memories like perfect photographs – there's always some fuzziness, some randomness in how memories are recalled and reconstructed. This turns out to be a feature, not a bug. It allows you to adapt memories to new situations, make creative connections, and generate new

insights. Modern AI systems are beginning to incorporate similar principles, moving away from rigid, exact
storage toward more flexible, noise-influenced representations.

What we're discovering is that randomness, properly
controlled, might be essential for any system – biological
or artificial – that needs to be truly creative and adaptive.
A neuroscientist might put it this way: "The brain isn't
noisy despite being intelligent; it's intelligent because
it's noisy." This insight is pushing AI development in
exciting new directions, suggesting that the path to more
creative and flexible AI systems might not lie in eliminating noise, but in learning to harness it just as our
brains do.

The next time your hand wobbles while holding that
coffee cup, or your mind wanders during a brainstorming
session, remember: that randomness isn't a bug in your
system – it's a feature that helps make you creative,
adaptive, and intelligent. And it might just hold the
key to building better AI.

Weather patterns and chaos theory

Imagine you're planning an outdoor wedding for next month. You check the weather forecast, but beyond a few days, it becomes more like educated guessing. Why can't our most powerful supercomputers, running sophisticated weather models, tell us if it will rain on your special day? The answer lies in a fascinating discovery that changed our understanding of not just weather, but the fundamental limits of prediction – including what we can expect from artificial intelligence.

The story begins in 1961, when meteorologist Edward Lorenz was running weather simulations on an early computer. One day, he took a shortcut by rounding some numbers to three decimal places instead of six – a difference so tiny it seemed meaningless, like worrying whether a butterfly's wingbeat in Brazil could affect the weather in Texas. To his astonishment, this microscopic change completely transformed his weather prediction. The "butterfly effect" was born, and with it came a profound insight about the limits of predictability in complex systems.

Think of it like this: imagine rolling a marble down a complex track with lots of branches and forks. If you release the marble from exactly the same spot each time, it follows the same path. But move your starting point by just a hair's width, and the marble might take a completely different route. Weather works similarly, but with millions of "marbles" all influencing each other's paths. This same principle affects any complex system – from weather patterns to financial markets to human behavior – and it poses a fundamental challenge for AI systems trying to make predictions.

Modern AI faces the same challenge as weather forecasters: the butterfly effect means that tiny uncertainties in our measurements or initial conditions can lead to vastly different outcomes. Just as we can't predict exact weather conditions months ahead, AI systems struggle to make long-term predictions about complex systems like stock markets, social trends, or human behavior. The more variables involved and the further into the future we try to predict, the more our uncertainty multiplies.

But here's where it gets interesting: while we can't predict exactly where each marble will end up, we might notice that they tend to collect in certain areas more than others. Weather follows similar patterns – we can't predict precise conditions months ahead, but we know that Seattle will probably be rainy in November and Dallas will likely be hot in July. Scientists call these patterns "strange attractors" – islands of predictability in an ocean of chaos. This insight has profound implications for AI: instead of seeking perfect predictions, we might need to focus on understanding these broader patterns and tendencies.

This mix of unpredictability and pattern shows up everywhere in nature. Watch smoke rise from a candle – at first it moves straight up, then suddenly breaks into swirling patterns that never exactly repeat but somehow look familiar. Or look at how crowds move through a busy station – chaotic yet following recognizable patterns. Nature seems to dance between order and chaos, creating complexity that's neither completely random nor fully predictable. AI systems must learn to dance this same dance.

Modern weather forecasters have learned to embrace this uncertainty, and AI developers are following suit. Instead of trying to make single, precise predictions, weather models now run many slightly different simulations – like rolling that marble dozens of times with tiny variations in the starting point. This gives them a range of possible outcomes, leading to predictions like "60% chance of rain." Similarly, advanced AI systems are moving away from trying to make exact predictions and instead working with probabilities and ranges of possible outcomes.

This shift in approach represents a fundamental change in how we think about artificial intelligence. Early AI researchers dreamed of creating systems that could calculate everything precisely, like a giant chess computer planning every move perfectly. But chaos theory teaches us that such perfect prediction is impossible for many real-world situations. Instead, truly intelligent systems need to be comfortable with uncertainty and able to adapt when things don't go as expected.

The implications reach far beyond weather prediction. When AI systems try to predict election outcomes, market trends, or human behavior, they face the same fundamental limitations that weather forecasters do. Small changes or overlooked variables can cascade into major differences in outcomes. This doesn't mean prediction is impossible, but it does mean we need to be realistic about what AI can achieve. The goal isn't perfect prediction – it's useful prediction within understood limits.

The weather remains our greatest teacher in this regard. Every time we check the forecast, we're reminded that even with all our technology and knowledge, some things remain fundamentally unpredictable. Yet within this uncertainty, we find useful patterns and meaningful predictions. It's not about controlling chaos – it's about understanding its boundaries and working within them.

This lesson is crucial for the future of AI. As we develop more powerful systems, we must remember that increased computing power alone won't overcome the fundamental limits of prediction in complex systems. The key to more effective AI might not lie in fighting against chaos, but in learning to work with it – just as weather forecasters have learned to do. In both weather and AI, sometimes the smartest approach is not to seek perfect prediction, but to embrace uncertainty as a fundamental part of how complex systems work.

Complex systems emerging from random interactions

Picture yourself in a stadium during a crowded sporting event. Suddenly, a wave of people standing and sitting ripples through the crowd. No one's in charge, no one planned it, yet this complex pattern emerges spontaneously from thousands of people each following a simple rule: "stand up when your neighbors do." This seemingly magical emergence of order from chaos isn't just a human phenomenon – it's one of nature's favorite tricks, and it might hold the key to understanding how artificial intelligence can surprise us with unexpected abilities.

Let's dive deep into the fascinating world of ant colonies. Each ant follows surprisingly simple rules: "if you find food, lay down a chemical trail on your way back; if you smell a strong trail, follow it; if you meet another ant, touch antennae to share information; if you find a dead nestmate, carry it to the cemetery area." No individual ant knows it's participating in sophisticated agriculture, yet somehow the colony cultivates fungus gardens, carefully controlling temperature and humidity. They can't comprehend warfare, yet armies of ants coordinate complex tactical maneuvers. Without any architectural training, they build ventilation systems that maintain perfect climate control. When disease breaks out, they implement quarantine procedures that human cities would envy.

What's remarkable is how these complex behaviors emerge from simple interactions. When an ant finds a good food source, it leaves a stronger chemical trail, which attracts more ants, who leave more chemicals – a feedback loop that quickly recruits the right number of foragers. If too many ants follow the trail, they exhaust the food source, the chemical trail evaporates, and the system self-corrects. No ant understands these population dynamics, yet the colony perfectly allocates its workforce.

This emergent complexity mirrors what we're discovering in deep learning systems. Just as no ant knows it's creating a sophisticated agricultural system, no single artificial neuron in a deep learning network understands the task it's solving. Yet from millions of simple connections adjusting their weights through feedback, remarkable abilities emerge. A neural network trained to recognize images might spontaneously develop internal layers that detect edges, then shapes, then complex features – a hierarchical organization that wasn't explicitly programmed.

The same magic happens in our cities and markets, but with even more surprising results. No central planner coordinates the food supply for a city of millions. Instead, countless independent decisions – a farmer choosing crops based on last year's prices, a grocer ordering stock based on local preferences, a consumer picking tonight's dinner – somehow create a robust, adaptive system. When trouble hits one supply chain, the system reorganizes like a living organism healing a wound.

The Internet grew this way too, and its evolution offers striking parallels to how deep learning networks develop. While engineers designed basic protocols for how computers should communicate, no one planned its current structure. Yet through millions of local decisions – where to place servers, how to route traffic, which connections to strengthen – the network evolved an architecture that's remarkably efficient and resilient. Similarly, when we train AI systems, we often find they discover solutions we never imagined, developing their own internal "protocols" for solving problems.

Nature's recipe for self-organization provides clues about why deep learning can generate unexpected capabilities. You need many simple elements (neurons in AI, ants in colonies), ways for success to reinforce itself (strengthening useful neural connections, reinforcing productive ant trails), and mechanisms to prevent single patterns from dominating (neural pruning, resource limitations in ant colonies). Add the ability for local actions to influence neighbors, and surprisingly sophisticated behaviors can emerge.

This insight is transforming how we approach artificial intelligence. Instead of trying to program every capability, we're creating environments where intelligence can emerge through training and interaction. Modern language models, for instance, develop abilities their creators didn't explicitly program – from solving logic puzzles to writing creative fiction. Like an ant colony developing agriculture without understanding farming, these systems discover solutions that surprise even their designers.

Think of it like the difference between building a bridge and growing a tree. Engineers must calculate every detail of a bridge's structure, but a tree grows into a robust form through countless local interactions following simple genetic rules. Similarly, while early AI researchers tried to program every aspect of intelligence, modern approaches focus on creating learning systems that can develop their own capabilities through training and interaction.

This emergent approach explains why AI systems sometimes develop unexpected abilities – both positive and potentially concerning. Just as ant colonies occasionally develop behaviors that seem almost bizarre (like creating living bridges or rafts), AI systems might discover solutions that we never anticipated. A system trained to play games might invent entirely new strategies, or a language model might develop unexpected ways of parsing and generating text.

The implications are profound. We might not need to fully understand intelligence to create AI systems that surpass human abilities in specific domains. Just as ant colonies achieve complex engineering feats without any individual ant understanding architecture, AI systems might solve problems in ways that we can't fully comprehend. This suggests both exciting possibilities and important challenges – how do we ensure these emergent behaviors align with our intentions?

Whether we're observing the intricate dance of an ant colony, the invisible hand of markets, or the emerging capabilities of AI systems, the message is clear: complex, intelligent behavior doesn't always need a central controller or explicit programming. Sometimes the most sophisticated solutions emerge from simple rules played out countless times through interaction and adaptation. This principle might be the key to developing AI systems that not only match but potentially exceed human capabilities in unexpected ways.

The Dance of Chaos and Order

Throughout this chapter, we've explored a counterintuitive truth: randomness isn't the enemy of intelligence – it's one of its essential ingredients. From the creative noise in our neural circuits to the unpredictable butterfly effects in weather systems, from the emergence of ant colony intelligence to the surprising capabilities of deep learning networks, we've seen how uncertainty and chaos play crucial roles in both natural and artificial intelligence.

Think of jazz improvisation. A classical piece follows a strict score, while jazz emerges from the interplay between structure and spontaneity. The best jazz isn't purely random, nor is it completely predetermined – it dances between chaos and order. Nature seems to prefer this jazz-like approach. Our brains don't compute like calculators; they thrive on a carefully balanced mix of reliability and randomness. Ant colonies don't follow rigid blueprints; they adapt and innovate through countless random interactions. Even the weather, in its endless complexity, reveals patterns within its chaos.

This understanding fundamentally changes how we think about artificial intelligence. Early AI researchers tried to build systems like classical orchestras – every note planned, every outcome predetermined. But nature suggests a different path: systems that thrive on the edge of chaos, where randomness and order meet. Modern AI is beginning to embrace this approach, incorporating controlled uncertainty in its algorithms, allowing for emergent behaviors, and developing probabilistic rather than deterministic solutions.

The results are striking. AI systems that incorporate strategic randomness often outperform their more rigid counterparts. They're more creative, finding novel solutions that purely deterministic approaches miss. They're more robust, adapting to unexpected situations rather than breaking when reality doesn't match their programming. They're more natural in their interactions, avoiding the robotic predictability that often betrays artificial systems.

But perhaps most intriguingly, these systems can surprise us. Just as the random interactions of ants can produce unexpected yet effective solutions to complex problems, AI systems incorporating controlled chaos can develop capabilities their creators never explicitly programmed. They can discover new strategies in games, find novel patterns in data, or develop unexpected approaches to problem-solving.

This suggests a profound shift in how we might achieve artificial general intelligence. Instead of trying to program intelligence directly – like trying to write a perfect score for every possible situation – we might need to create systems that can jazz with reality, systems that use randomness as a tool for exploration and adaptation. The goal isn't to eliminate uncertainty, but to harness it, to find the sweet spot between chaos and order where true intelligence emerges.

As we move forward, this insight opens up exciting questions. How can we better understand the relationship between randomness and creativity? What's the right balance between chaos and order in intelligent systems? How can we ensure that emergent AI behaviors align with our goals while still allowing for beneficial surprises? These questions will guide us into the next chapter, where we'll explore how embracing uncertainty might be key not just to building better AI, but to understanding intelligence itself.

The lesson from nature is clear: the path to robust, adaptable intelligence doesn't lie in eliminating randomness, but in learning to dance with it. In this dance between chaos and order, we might find the key to creating AI systems that don't just compute, but truly think – systems that don't just follow rules, but create and discover. The future of AI might not lie in perfect prediction and control, but in mastering this delicate dance between randomness and structure, between the known and the unknown.

References & Sources

Evolution and Random Mutation

Chance and Necessity: An Essay on the Natural Philosophy of Modern Biology

Jacques Monod

Alfred A. Knopf, 1971

Explores the fundamental role of chance in biological evolution and its relationship with natural selection.

Neural Noise in Brain Function

Noise in the nervous system

A. Aldo Faisal, Luc P.J. Selen, and Daniel M. Wolpert

Nature Reviews Neuroscience, 2008

Presents groundbreaking research on how neural noise contributes positively to brain function and decision-making processes.

Weather and Chaos Theory

Chaos: Making a New Science

James Gleick

Viking Books, 1987

Chronicles Edward Lorenz's discovery of chaos theory through weather pattern studies, including the famous "butterfly effect."

Emergence in Complex Systems

At Home in the Universe: The Search for Laws of Self-Organization and Complexity

Stuart Kauffman

Oxford University Press, 1995

Examines how order emerges from random interactions in complex systems, from biology to economics.

Order and Chaos Balance

The Quark and the Jaguar: Adventures in the Simple and the Complex

Murray Gell-Mann

W.H. Freeman, 1994

Explores the interplay between chaos and order in natural systems, from particle physics to evolutionary biology.

Embracing Uncertainty

Introduction to probabilistic thinking

Imagine playing chess with a five-year-old who insists on absolute certainty about every move. "Is this the best move? Yes or no?" they demand. You might struggle to answer because chess, like most real-world situations, rarely offers such clear-cut choices. This childlike insistence on certainty mirrors the early days of artificial intelligence, when researchers thought building smart machines meant programming them with rigid rules and absolute truths.

But our daily lives reveal a different kind of intelligence – one built on maybes rather than absolutes. Watch yourself during a typical morning: You check the weather forecast and decide whether to take an umbrella (30% chance of rain? Better safe than sorry). You glance at traffic on your phone and estimate whether your usual route will get you to work on time. At the coffee shop, you quickly gauge which line will move faster based on dozens of subtle cues – how many people look ready to order, whether someone might be picking up a large office order, if the barista seems experienced.

Consider how you navigate a crowded sidewalk. You're constantly processing a stream of probabilistic predictions: that person is probably turning left based on their head position, those friends walking together will likely maintain their formation, that cyclist might swerve to avoid the puddle. Your brain juggles hundreds of these maybes every minute, adjusting them continuously as new information arrives. You're not solving complex physics equations – you're surfing a wave of probabilities.

Or think about how you understand speech in different contexts. At a quiet dinner, you easily follow the conversation. In a noisy restaurant, you might catch only 60% of the words, but your brain fills in the gaps by calculating the most probable meanings. At a concert, you might understand someone even when you hear only every third word, because your brain is constantly generating and updating predictions about what they're likely saying.

The shift becomes even clearer when we watch how humans handle uncertainty in social situations. Imagine you're at a party and someone tells a joke. You don't just process the words – you're simultaneously estimating whether others found it funny, whether it might have offended anyone, whether it's appropriate to laugh out loud or just smile. Every social interaction involves dozens of these rapid probability calculations: Is my friend's "fine" actually fine? Does that slight pause in my boss's email suggest concern? Should I interpret that ambiguous text message literally or sarcastically?

This natural probabilistic thinking turns out to be

far more powerful than rigid logic for dealing with real-world complexity. Early AI researchers tried to program computers with strict rules: "IF someone says 'fine' AND their tone is flat, THEN they are not actually fine." But this approach quickly broke down in the messy reality of human interaction. Modern AI systems, like humans, work with probabilities: this tone of voice suggests a 70% chance of frustration, that choice of words implies a 85% probability of sarcasm.

The shift offers three powerful advantages. First, it mirrors reality – few things in life are completely certain, and systems that acknowledge this tend to make better decisions. When you're driving and see a ball roll into the street, you don't wait for absolute certainty that a child will follow it – you slow down based on the probability. Second, it's remarkably robust – even with incomplete or noisy information, probabilistic systems can still function effectively, just as you can follow a conversation even when a bus drives by. Third, it creates a natural framework for learning – when you're wrong about something, you don't have to completely rebuild your understanding; you simply adjust your probabilities.

Modern AI systems have embraced this probabilistic revolution. When your phone recognizes your speech, it's not making binary decisions about each sound – it's weighing probabilities, considering context, and making educated guesses. When a self-driving car navigates traffic, it's constantly calculating probability distributions about other vehicles' likely movements. When an AI language model suggests the next word as you type, it's predicting probabilities based on context, not following rigid grammar rules.

Perhaps most intriguingly, this shift has changed how we understand human intelligence itself. Our brains appear to be sophisticated probability engines rather than logic computers. Every perception, decision, and action emerges from a complex web of probabilistic predictions, continuously updated based on experience. When you catch a ball, you're not solving differential equations – you're running countless probabilistic simulations shaped by years of experience. When you recognize a friend's face in a crowd, you're not performing pixel-perfect matching – you're making probability-based predictions about patterns and features.

This probabilistic revolution brought two particularly powerful frameworks to the forefront: Bayesian reasoning and Hidden Markov Models (HMMs). Bayesian reasoning formalized how we should update our beliefs based on new evidence – much like how you naturally revise your opinion about a restaurant as you hear more reviews from friends. Hidden Markov Models offered a way to understand sequences where we can only observe indirect effects – like how you infer someone's emotional state from their tone of voice and body language, without directly seeing their feelings.

Together, these frameworks highlight a crucial insight: intelligence isn't about finding absolute truth, but about making good decisions with incomplete information. Whether we're understanding speech, diagnosing diseases, or predicting weather, success comes not from eliminating uncertainty, but from embracing and managing it effectively. This represents a fundamental shift away from the dream of perfect, deterministic AI toward systems that, like humans, thrive in a world of probabilities.

Bayesian Thinking: The Science of Uncertainty

Imagine you're walking down a street and hear hoofbeats. In Kansas, you'd probably think "horse." In Manhattan, you'd think "police horse." In Africa, you might think "zebra." Without realizing it, you're using Bayesian reasoning – starting with what you know about where you are (your "prior" beliefs) and combining it with new evidence (the sound of hoofbeats) to reach a conclusion.

This natural process of updating beliefs based on new evidence is the essence of Bayesian reasoning, named after Thomas Bayes, an 18th-century minister who first formalized these ideas. It's something we do instinctively hundreds of times a day. When you're driving and see brake lights ahead, your brain instantly combines multiple pieces of information: the time of day (rush hour?), the location (near a school?), recent weather (wet roads?), to estimate the likelihood of a serious slowdown. Each new piece of information updates your prediction.

Consider how a doctor diagnoses strep throat. They start with base rates – maybe 20% of sore throats in winter are strep (the prior probability). Then they see white spots on the tonsils. From experience, they know that 80% of strep cases have white spots, while only 20% of non-strep sore throats do (the likelihood ratio).

Combining these pieces of information dramatically increases the probability of strep. If a rapid strep test then comes back positive, the probability jumps even higher, since these tests rarely give false positives. This isn't just casual updating – it follows precise mathematical rules that tell us exactly how to weigh old beliefs against new evidence.

We use this same process in social situations. Imagine you text a friend "Are you okay?" and they respond "I'm fine." Your brain instantly combines multiple priors: how this friend usually communicates, recent events in their life, the delay before their response, whether they added an exclamation point or period. Based on these, you might conclude they're actually upset (despite saying "fine"), somewhat annoyed, or genuinely okay. As you interact more, each response updates your assessment.

The power of Bayesian reasoning becomes clear when we see how it's transformed different fields:

In medicine, it revolutionized diagnosis. Instead of treating each symptom as a yes/no checkbox, modern diagnostic systems use Bayesian networks to consider how symptoms interact. When IBM's Watson diagnoses patients, it starts with base rates of different conditions, then updates these probabilities based on symptoms, test results, age, gender, and medical history. This approach outperforms traditional diagnostic methods, especially for rare or complex conditions.

In spam filtering, Bayesian methods created a break-through. Earlier filters used rigid rules ("block emails containing 'viagra'"), which spammers easily evaded. Bayesian filters instead learn from experience, calculating the probability of an email being spam based on all its characteristics – words, formatting, sending time, links. They adapt as spam tactics change and customize to each user's email patterns. Gmail's spam filter, using these principles, blocks over 99.9% of spam while having very few false positives.

Self-driving cars use Bayesian reasoning to navigate safely. When a Tesla sees a ball roll into the street, it combines multiple probabilities: How likely is a child to follow the ball? What's the probability of someone emerging from between those parked cars? How likely are other drivers to stop suddenly? Each sensor reading updates these probabilities, helping the car make split-second decisions about slowing down or swerving.

In scientific research, Bayesian methods have transformed how we interpret data. Traditional statistics ask "What's the probability of seeing this data if my hypothesis is true?" leading to often-misinterpreted p-values. Bayesian analysis instead asks "What's the probability my hypothesis is true given this data?" This approach has resolved long-standing controversies in fields from psychology to physics. For example, the discovery of the Higgs boson used Bayesian methods to combine data from millions of particle collisions, each updating the probability of the particle's existence.

Recommendation systems use Bayesian reasoning to suggest products or content. When Netflix recommends shows, it's not just matching categories – it's constantly updating probabilities based on your viewing patterns, similar users' preferences, time of day, device you're using, and dozens of other factors. Each click or viewing session refines these predictions.

Even artificial intelligence researchers have embraced Bayesian principles. Modern language models like GPT use Bayesian-inspired techniques to predict the most likely next word given the context. Image recognition systems use Bayesian networks to combine low-level visual features into high-level understanding, much like our brains do.

Perhaps most importantly, Bayesian reasoning offers a framework for rational thinking in an uncertain world. It tells us exactly how strongly we should hold beliefs and how much we should update them given new evidence. It suggests that strongly held beliefs should change only with strong evidence, while tentative beliefs might shift substantially with modest evidence. This mathematical framework for changing one's mind has profound implications for everything from scientific research to public debate.

Consider how this applies to evaluating news. Your

prior belief about a claim might depend on the source's reliability history. Each additional source, fact-check, or piece of evidence updates this probability. Extraordinary claims (like breakthrough medical cures) require extraordinary evidence to overcome low prior probabilities. This approach helps navigate between blind acceptance and rigid skepticism.

The legacy of Bayesian reasoning extends beyond its mathematical applications. It provides a philosophical framework for rational thinking under uncertainty, a guide for updating beliefs in light of evidence, and a reminder that knowledge is usually probabilistic rather than absolute. In a world where we're constantly bombarded with new information, these principles offer a powerful tool for thinking clearly about what we know, what we don't know, and how new evidence should change our minds.

Hidden Markov Models: The Silent Revolution

Have you ever wondered how your phone understands your voice commands, or how streaming services figure out what songs you might like? Behind many of these everyday technologies lies a clever mathematical tool called a Hidden Markov Model, or HMM. Don't let the fancy name intimidate you – the basic idea is as simple as playing detective with patterns.

Let's break it down: "Hidden" means we're trying to figure out something we can't see directly. "Markov" (named after mathematician Andrey Markov) means what happens next depends mainly on what's happening right now. And "Model" just means it's a way of representing how things work. Put them together, and you have a method for making smart guesses about hidden situations based on the clues we can observe.

Here's a simple example: Imagine trying to guess what your neighbor is cooking based only on the smells wafting through the wall. First, you catch a whiff of garlic and olive oil sautéing. "Italian?" you wonder. Then comes the aroma of curry powder. Suddenly, you change your prediction to Indian cuisine. This everyday guessing game perfectly illustrates how Hidden Markov Models work.

In this case, the actual cooking process (chopping, sautéing, simmering) is hidden from view – you can't see into your neighbor's kitchen. But the smells you detect are clues that help you guess what's really happening. Your brain naturally updates its predictions as new evidence (smells) arrives. This is exactly what Hidden Markov Models do, just more systematically and with mathematics.

Think of Hidden Markov Models as detective tools that help us figure out what's really happening (the hidden part) by looking at the clues we can observe. This simple but powerful idea transformed everything from how our phones understand speech to how scientists find genes in DNA.

HMMs solve three basic detective problems we face all the time:

- "What's probably happening?" Like guessing whether your neighbor is making pasta or curry based on a sequence of smells.

- "What steps led to this?" Like working backward from the smells to figure out exactly what cooking steps your neighbor followed.

- "How can we get better at guessing?" Like learning from past cooking sessions to make better predictions next time.

The biggest success story came from speech recognition. Before HMMs, computers were terrible at understanding speech because everyone talks differently. Even the same person says the same word differently when they're excited, tired, or have a cold. HMMs cracked this problem by treating speech like a guessing game: "What words would most likely create these sound patterns?" This breakthrough is why your phone can now understand you pretty well, even with background noise or an accent.

This success sparked a chain reaction across different fields. Biologists realized they could use the same trick to find genes in DNA – treating genes as the "hidden recipe" that creates the DNA patterns we can see. Security cameras used HMMs to track people moving through spaces, like following a story based on snapshots. Financial analysts used them to spot hidden patterns in stock prices.

But making HMMs work in the real world wasn't easy. Imagine trying to predict everything someone might cook – the number of possible recipes and cooking steps quickly becomes overwhelming. Speech recognition faced similar challenges: thousands of possible words, endless ways to pronounce them, different accents, background noise. Engineers had to get creative:

- They grouped similar things together, like treating similar-sounding word pronunciations as the same

- They broke big problems into smaller pieces, like understanding sentences part by part

- They used powerful computers and clever short-cuts to make predictions faster

- They gathered huge amounts of example data to train their systems

As technology improved, so did HMMs. They got better at handling complex patterns, like understanding both individual cooking steps and entire recipes at once. They learned to combine different types of clues – like using both smell and sound to guess what's cooking. When smartphones came along, engineers found ways to make HMMs work quickly on small devices.

Today, HMMs are everywhere, quietly working behind the scenes. They help:

- Your phone understand your voice commands

- Security systems track movement

- Scientists analyze DNA

- Doctors interpret medical signals

- Financial systems spot market trends

Perhaps the biggest lesson from HMMs is that sometimes the best way to handle uncertainty isn't to eliminate it, but to embrace it. Instead of trying to make rigid rules for every possible situation, HMMs succeed by carefully weighing probabilities and updating their guesses as new information arrives.

This idea changed how we think about artificial intelligence. It showed that machines don't need to think exactly like humans to solve complex problems. Sometimes, having a good framework for making educated guesses is more powerful than trying to create detailed rules for every situation.

As we push into new frontiers of AI, from self-driving cars to medical diagnosis systems, the lessons from HMMs remain valuable: embrace uncertainty, look for patterns in data, and keep solutions practical. Their success reminds us that sometimes the most powerful ideas are like good detectives – they might not see everything directly, but they know how to follow the clues.

Case study: Speech recognition break-through

Remember our discussion about why early speech recognition systems failed so spectacularly? Those ambitious engineers in the 1960s thought they had found the perfect solution: if they could identify aircraft from radar signatures, surely they could identify words from sound waves. Their template-matching approach seemed beautifully logical - analyze sound waves for distinct acoustic features, then match these patterns against templates of known words. Like matching a song to sheet music. Simple, elegant, and as we saw earlier, destined for failure.

But knowing why something failed isn't the same as knowing how to fix it. The fundamental challenge we discussed - that speech patterns vary enormously even for the same word - remained a stubborn obstacle. Engineers needed a completely different way of thinking about the problem.

This is where our story takes an unexpected turn. Instead of trying harder to perfect template matching, some researchers started asking a different question altogether. What if, rather than asking "What does this sound wave look like?", we asked "What sequence of words most likely generated these sounds?" This subtle shift in perspective would prove revolutionary.

Remember our earlier example of "I read a red book"? We saw how template matching crashed and burned when faced with this seemingly simple phrase. The same word "read" could be pronounced two different ways, "red" and "read" could sound identical, and word boundaries blurred in continuous speech. Traditional systems were like a student mechanically comparing answers to an answer key - they could only handle exact matches.

Enter Hidden Markov Models (HMMs). Rather than fighting against speech's inherent variability, HMMs embraced it. They approached speech recognition like a detective story, where each sound offered clues to the words being spoken, and context provided crucial evidence for interpretation. This was exactly the kind of flexible, context-aware approach we saw was missing in those early systems.

The technical machinery behind this probabilistic approach was elegant and powerful. HMMs modeled speech recognition using two key elements: hidden states (the actual words or phonemes being spoken) and observable emissions (the measurable acoustic features). Think of it like a mystery novel where you can't directly observe the criminal's actions (hidden states) but can see their effects (observable emissions).

The system maintained three crucial probability distributions that worked together like characters in our detective story. First, the initial probabilities told us where sequences typically start - like knowing that "I" is a common way to begin a sentence. Second, transition probabilities tracked how states follow each other - capturing the knowledge that after "I", a verb like "read" is more likely than an adjective like "red". Finally, emission probabilities connected each state to the sounds it typically produces - the acoustic signature of each word.

Returning to our challenging sentence "I read a red book", the HMM approach shines. At the beginning, the high initial probability of "I" gives it a strong start. After "I", the transition probabilities favor "read" as a verb. Following "a", those same transition probabilities now prefer "red" as an adjective. Each decision influences the next, creating a coherent interpretation of the entire utterance.

The mathematical detective work reaches its peak with three fundamental problems that HMMs had to solve: evaluation (how likely is this sequence?), decoding (what's the most likely sequence of states?), and learning (how to determine the model parameters from training data?). The Viterbi algorithm, a particularly clever piece of mathematical deduction, efficiently finds the most likely sequence of words by considering all possible paths through the state space simultaneously.

This probabilistic approach proved superior to template matching in every way. It could handle natural variations in speech because it wasn't looking for exact matches. It used context through transition probabilities to disambiguate similar-sounding words. It could learn and improve from data, adapting to new speakers and conditions. Perhaps most importantly, it could process continuous speech without needing clear word boundaries.

As speech recognition evolved, particularly with the rise of deep learning, the implementation became more sophisticated while preserving these fundamental insights. Modern systems typically employ deep neural networks, especially recurrent neural networks and transformers, which can capture longer-range dependencies than traditional HMMs. These newer architectures maintain probability distributions, but they're richer and more nuanced.

Looking at our example sentence through modern eyes, the system now considers an impressive array of evidence. If someone mentioned "reading" earlier in the conversation, that influences the interpretation of "read." Speaker identification helps adapt to individual voices. Ambient noise conditions inform confidence levels. Topic context and user history provide additional clues. The system can even learn from real-time feedback, continuously improving its performance.

Perhaps most remarkably, modern systems can learn

end-to-end, directly mapping audio to text without explicitly modeling intermediate states. They can discover patterns that designers might never have considered, leading to levels of accuracy that seemed impossible in the early days of speech recognition.

Yet amid all these advances, the core insight from HMMs remains valid: embracing uncertainty through probabilistic modeling works better than trying to make deterministic decisions. The main difference is that modern systems can handle this uncertainty in more sophisticated ways, considering evidence from many sources and maintaining complex probability distributions over possible interpretations.

The journey from simple template matching through HMMs to today's deep learning systems tells us something profound about artificial intelligence. Sometimes the key to solving a problem isn't to eliminate uncertainty, but to embrace it mathematically. By learning to think in probabilities rather than certainties, speech recognition transformed from a frustrated pattern-matching exercise into one of AI's greatest success stories.

This breakthrough didn't just solve the problems we discussed earlier - it fundamentally changed how we approach artificial intelligence. The success of HMMs showed that embracing uncertainty through mathematical probability often works better than trying to make rigid, deterministic decisions. This insight has influenced nearly every aspect of modern AI, from computer vision to language translation to robotics. What started as a better way to recognize speech became a whole new way of thinking about machine intelligence.

From Probability to Neural Networks

Our exploration of uncertainty reasoning and Bayesian methods reveals a crucial insight: real-world problems rarely have clear-cut answers. Whether we're diagnosing diseases, recognizing speech, or making predictions, success often comes from embracing uncertainty and thinking probabilistically. This perspective transformed artificial intelligence from brittle, rule-based systems into more robust probabilistic ones.

We saw this transformation clearly in speech recognition, where Hidden Markov Models revolutionized the field by replacing rigid pattern matching with probabilistic sequence modeling. HMMs demonstrated how embracing uncertainty - treating speech recognition as probability distributions rather than exact matches - could tackle problems that seemed intractable with traditional approaches.

However, HMMs had their own limitations. They required experts to carefully design probability distributions and specify which features of the input data were important. For speech recognition, this meant manually crafting acoustic features like frequency patterns, energy distributions, and temporal characteristics. As tasks became more complex, this manual feature engineering became a bottleneck. The uncertainty in real-world data was simply too complex to capture with hand-designed probability distributions.

This challenge wasn't unique to speech recognition. Across many domains, AI systems were hitting similar walls - they needed more sophisticated ways to handle uncertainty and randomness than humans could design by hand. The field needed approaches that could automatically learn complex probability distributions from data.

The solution would come from an unexpected direction: a revival of neural networks, leading to what we now call deep learning. But here's the fascinating part - randomness and uncertainty would play an even more crucial role in these new systems. Not only would they output probability distributions like their predecessors, but they would also use randomness in fundamental new ways during their training and operation.

In the next chapters, we'll discover how embracing randomness even more deeply through deep learning triggered a new AI revolution. We'll see how incorporating uncertainty at every level - from network initialization to training procedures to output distributions - led to breakthroughs that transformed the field. And we'll explore how this culminated in systems like ChatGPT, which represent perhaps the most sophisticated application yet of probabilistic thinking in artificial intelligence.

References & Sources

Probabilistic AI Revolution

Artificial Intelligence: A Modern Approach
Stuart Russell and Peter Norvig
Pearson, 4th Edition, 2021
Documents the paradigm shift from logic-based to probabilistic approaches in AI, marking a fundamental change in the field.

Bayesian Methods in AI

Probabilistic Reasoning in Intelligent Systems: Networks of Plausible Inference
Judea Pearl
Morgan Kaufmann, 1988
Presents the foundational work on Bayesian networks and their application to artificial intelligence.

Hidden Markov Models Revolution

A Tutorial on Hidden Markov Models and Selected Applications in Speech Recognition
Lawrence R. Rabiner
Proceedings of the IEEE, 1989
Details the breakthrough applications of HMMs in speech recognition, which transformed the field.

Speech Recognition Breakthrough

A Historical Perspective of Speech Recognition
Xuedong Huang, James Baker, and Raj Reddy
Communications of the ACM, 2014
Chronicles the pivotal transition from rule-based to statistical methods in speech recognition technology.

Neural-Probabilistic Integration

Deep Learning

Ian Goodfellow, Yoshua Bengio, and Aaron Courville

MIT Press, 2016

Examines the convergence of probabilistic methods and neural networks, creating more powerful hybrid approaches.

The Deep Learning Revolution

Neural networks and random initialization

One of the most counterintuitive aspects of deep learning's success is that it begins with pure uncertainty. When we initialize a neural network, we start by assigning random weights to all connections. This seems like a strange way to build an intelligent system—imagine trying to solve a complex problem by starting with random guesses. Yet this apparent chaos holds the key to how modern artificial intelligence learns.

To understand why this works, let's start with something familiar: how a child learns to recognize cats. We don't teach children by giving them a rulebook about whisker lengths, ear shapes, and fur patterns. Instead, they start with no preconceptions and learn through experience, gradually developing their own understanding of what makes a cat a cat. Neural networks work in a surprisingly similar way, but their "blank slate" takes the form of random numbers.

But what exactly is a neural network? Imagine a vast web of connected points, like stars connected by invisible threads. Each point can light up based on signals it receives from other points through these threads. Some connections are stronger than others, like thick ropes versus thin strings, and these connection strengths—what we call weights—determine everything about how the network processes information. When you show an image to a neural network, this web of connections transforms the raw pixel data through multiple layers, eventually lighting up specific points that represent what the network "thinks" it's seeing.

The magic—and the mystery—lies in how these connections learn their proper strengths. In traditional computer programs, we tell the computer exactly what to do step by step. But with neural networks, we do something radically different: we start with random connection strengths and let the network figure out the right values through experience.

Just like a child learns by trial and error, neural networks learn by making mistakes and gradually correcting them. But how does this actually work? To understand this fascinating process, imagine you're blindfolded in a hilly landscape, trying to find the lowest point. You can't see where you're going, but you can feel the slope under your feet. Each step you take, you check which way the ground slopes downward and carefully move in that direction. This is essentially what neural networks do in a process called gradient descent—though instead of a physical landscape, they're exploring a vast mathematical space where each point represents one possible set of connection strengths.

When we start with random connections, it's like

dropping our blindfolded explorer at a random point in this landscape. Why random? Because we genuinely don't know where to start. If we always started at the same place, we might always end up in the same valley, missing deeper valleys elsewhere. By starting at different random points, we give our network multiple chances to find the best solution. It's like sending many explorers to different starting points—some might get stuck in shallow valleys, but others might find their way to deeper, better valleys.

The learning process itself is remarkably systematic despite starting from chaos. When shown a training example—say, a picture of a cat—the network first makes a guess based on its current random connections. Initially, these guesses are nonsense, like a child randomly pointing at things and saying "cat." But here's where it gets interesting: the network doesn't just guess and move on. It compares its guess to the correct answer and makes tiny adjustments to all its connections to do slightly better next time.

These adjustments are incredibly subtle. Imagine turning thousands of tiny knobs, each by just a fraction of a degree. Some connections get slightly stronger, others slightly weaker. Each adjustment is so small it seems meaningless, but over millions of examples, something remarkable happens: patterns begin to emerge from the chaos. It's like watching a photograph slowly come into focus, or seeing a sculpture gradually emerge from a formless block of clay.

What's truly fascinating is that different networks, started with different random connections, often discover similar patterns. In image recognition, for example, networks naturally learn to detect edges and shapes before moving on to more complex features—just like our own visual system. This suggests these patterns aren't arbitrary but reflect genuine structure in the world. The randomness hasn't led to chaos; it's led to discovery.

This mirrors what we're learning about how biological brains develop. While the basic architecture of our brains is genetically determined, the fine details of neural connections appear somewhat random at birth. These connections get refined through experience, just like our artificial networks. Nature seems to have discovered the same principle: starting with flexibility and uncertainty leads to better learning than starting with rigid, predetermined patterns.

This marks a profound shift from earlier approaches to artificial intelligence. Traditional AI systems, like the Hidden Markov Models we explored earlier, relied on carefully designed probability distributions. Experts had to explicitly tell these systems what patterns to look for and how to handle uncertainty. It was like trying to teach someone to recognize cats by giving them a detailed manual of cat features and measurements.

Deep learning turns this approach upside down. Instead of carefully designing uncertainty into the system, we embrace it completely at the start. We begin with maximum uncertainty—pure randomness—and let the system discover patterns on its own. This proves remarkably powerful because it can find patterns we might never think to program, and adapt to new patterns without being explicitly reprogrammed.

The implications go far beyond technical implementation. This process suggests something profound about the nature of intelligence itself. Rather than seeing intelligence as the product of careful design and predetermined knowledge, deep learning suggests it emerges from the ability to find patterns in chaos. It's not about starting with the right answers; it's about having the right learning process.

Think about how this changes our understanding of learning and intelligence. Traditional approaches tried to eliminate uncertainty, seeing it as an obstacle to be overcome. But deep learning's success suggests uncertainty might be essential to learning itself. Starting from randomness gives systems the flexibility to discover solutions we might never have imagined.

This insight has transformed not just how we build AI systems, but how we think about intelligence itself. The path to knowledge doesn't have to start with knowledge—it can start with uncertainty, curiosity, and the freedom to explore. In the chapters ahead, we'll see how this principle extends beyond neural networks to create some of the most remarkable AI systems ever built, including the language models that can now engage in sophisticated conversations with humans.

In a way, this mirrors the scientific process itself: progress often comes not from assuming we know the answers, but from embracing uncertainty and letting patterns emerge from careful observation and experimentation. Deep learning's success with random initialization reminds us that sometimes, the best way to find answers is to admit we don't know them in the first place.

Word embeddings revealing world knowledge

One of the most striking demonstrations of deep learning's power came from an unexpected source: the discovery that neural networks trained on text could automatically learn rich representations of meaning. These "word embeddings" revealed that networks could capture complex real-world relationships without ever being explicitly taught them. The story of how researchers stumbled upon this capability, and what it taught us about both language and intelligence, marks a fundamental shift in our approach to artificial intelligence.

The journey began with a deceptively simple question: how can we represent words in a way that captures their meaning? Traditional approaches used discrete symbols—essentially treating each word as an independent entity with no inherent relationship to any other word. This one-hot encoding, as it's called, represents each word as a vector of zeros with a single 1 in a unique position. In this scheme, "cat" and "kitten" are as different from each other as "cat" and "democracy." This clearly missed something fundamental about how language works.

The breakthrough came from an unexpected direction. Rather than trying to explicitly encode meaning, researchers wondered if meaning could emerge from patterns of word usage. The insight was profound in its simplicity: words that appear in similar contexts likely have related meanings. You might find "cat" and "dog" in similar contexts (pet, animal, veterinarian) while "democracy" appears in very different contexts (government, elections, freedom).

This idea led to the development of Word2Vec by Tomas Mikolov and his team at Google in 2013. The algorithm works by training a neural network on a surprisingly simple task: given a word, predict the words that appear near it in text (or vice versa). For instance, if the network sees the phrase "the cat sat on the," it might try to predict that "mat" is likely to appear next. Through millions of such predictions, the network gradually learns to represent each word as a dense vector of numbers—typically 100 to 300 dimensions—where similar words end up with similar vectors.

The training process itself is fascinating. The network starts with random vectors for each word, just as we saw with random initialization in the previous section. As it makes predictions and learns from its mistakes, it gradually adjusts these vectors. If "cat" and "dog" frequently appear in similar contexts, their vectors slowly align. The network isn't told anything about what words mean—it discovers these relationships purely from usage patterns.

The results were astonishing. When researchers examined the learned vectors, they found rich semantic structures that no one had explicitly programmed. Words clustered naturally into meaningful groups: animals together, countries together, numbers together. But that was just the beginning. The vectors captured sophisticated relationships that went far beyond simple similarity.

The most famous example is the discovery of analogy relationships. Researchers found that vector arithmetic produced meaningful results. The classic demonstration shows that if you take the vector for "king," subtract the vector for "man," and add the vector for "woman," you get a vector very close to that of "queen." The network had discovered gender relationships. Similar patterns emerged for countless other relationships:

$$Paris - France + Italy \approx Rome$$

$$walking - walked + run \approx ran$$

$$brother - man + woman \approx sister$$

$$Microsoft - Windows + Apple \approx MacOS$$

These weren't isolated examples or cherry-picked results. The embeddings captured systematic patterns across the entire vocabulary. They encoded that capitals are to countries as largest cities are to states. They learned that past tense transforms verbs in consistent ways. They captured that "expensive" relates to "luxury" as "cheap" relates to "budget."

The technical sophistication behind these results goes deeper than the basic Word2Vec model. Researchers developed various approaches to learning these embeddings, each with its own insights. GloVe (Global Vectors for Word Representation), developed at Stanford, looks at global word co-occurrence statistics rather than local context windows. FastText, created by Facebook Research, learns representations for subword units, allowing it to handle out-of-vocabulary words and capture morphological relationships.

These methods revealed different aspects of how meaning is encoded in language. Word2Vec excels at capturing semantic relationships through local context. GloVe better captures global statistical patterns. FastText shows how meaning can be compositional, built up from smaller units. Together, they demonstrated that language contains rich structures at multiple levels, all discoverable through pattern analysis.

The applications of these discoveries were immediate and far-reaching. Search engines could now understand that someone searching for "automobile issues" might be interested in pages about "car problems." Recommendation systems could suggest products based on semantic similarity rather than just literal keyword matches. Translation systems could map words between languages by learning that the relationship between "cat" and "kitten" in English paralleled the relationship between "chat" and "chaton" in French.

But the impact went beyond practical applications. These embeddings revealed surprising insights about language itself. They showed that words carry vast amounts of implicit knowledge in their usage patterns. Consider how much information is encoded in the contexts where we use words:

- "The cat ___ the mouse" (predator-prey relationship)

- "She poured the coffee into her ___" (container relationship)

- "The doctor prescribed ___ for the infection" (medical treatment relationship)

The embeddings learned all these relationships and more, simply by observing patterns in text. They learned that doctors treat patients, that coffee is hot and liquid, that cats chase mice—all without being explicitly told any of these facts.

This led to even more sophisticated applications. Medical researchers used embeddings to discover potential new drug interactions by analyzing patterns in scientific papers. Legal firms used them to better search through case law. Financial analysts used them to predict market movements by analyzing news articles. The embeddings weren't just capturing simple word relationships—they were encoding complex domain knowledge.

The technology proved particularly powerful in combination with other techniques. Modern language models like BERT and GPT use more sophisticated forms of embeddings that capture context-dependent meaning. These contextual embeddings recognize that words can have different meanings in different contexts: "bank" can refer to a financial institution or the edge of a river, and the embedding shifts accordingly.

But perhaps the most profound implications came from what these embeddings revealed about biases in language. Because they learn from human-generated text, they absorb human prejudices and stereotypes. Researchers found troubling patterns:

- Gender biases: "doctor" was more closely associated with male terms, "nurse" with female terms

- Racial biases: European names were more closely associated with positive words than African American names

- Age biases: "elderly" was associated more with negative terms than "young"

- Cultural biases: Western concepts were often treated as universal while non-Western concepts were marked as "other"

These weren't just abstract concerns. When word embeddings were used in applications like resume screening or loan approval systems, they could perpetuate and amplify these biases. A system using these embeddings might unconsciously rate resumes with female names as less suitable for technical positions, or consider minority applicants higher risk for loans, simply because these associations exist in the training data.

This revelation sparked important discussions about bias in AI systems. Researchers developed techniques to detect and mitigate these biases, but the challenge runs deep. The biases in embeddings reflect biases in society, captured through language. This raises profound questions about the relationship between language, thought, and social structures.

The bias problem also highlighted something remarkable about embeddings: they can capture subtle cultural knowledge and social dynamics. They learn that certain professions are prestigiouars with high education, while others are viewed as less skilled. They capture that some behaviors are considered polite in some cultures and rude in others. They even learn changing social attitudes over time when trained on historical texts.

This ability to absorb cultural knowledge led to interesting applications in social science research. Historians used embeddings to track how word meanings and associations changed over time. Sociologists used them to study how different groups use language differently. Anthropologists used them to analyze cultural differences in concept relationships.

The success of word embeddings also challenged fundamental assumptions about artificial intelligence. Traditional approaches tried to explicitly encode knowledge in formal logic or databases, assuming that was necessary for intelligent behavior. Word embeddings showed that knowledge could emerge naturally from learning statistical patterns. The network wasn't reasoning about relationships in any way we'd traditionally recognize—it was discovering them in the structure of language itself.

This insight has implications far beyond language processing. It suggests that many aspects of intelligence might emerge naturally from pattern recognition rather than explicit reasoning. Just as humans learn much of their world knowledge implicitly through language exposure, artificial systems might best acquire knowledge through discovering patterns rather than being explicitly programmed.

The technology continues to evolve. Modern transformers use attention mechanisms to create dynamic, context-aware embeddings. These can capture even more subtle relationships and handle ambiguity better than static embeddings. Some systems learn embeddings across multiple modalities, connecting language patterns to visual patterns or audio patterns.

Yet the core insight remains revolutionary: meaning emerges from patterns. We don't need to explicitly program knowledge into machines. If we give them enough examples and the right learning architecture, they can discover these patterns on their own. This principle has become central to modern artificial intelligence, extending far beyond language to areas like image recognition, scientific discovery, and creative generation.

How "black box" captured real-world relationships

The success of deep learning presented AI researchers with a fascinating paradox. These systems were simultaneously more opaque and more effective than their predecessors. Unlike traditional AI systems, where each rule and decision boundary was explicitly programmed, deep neural networks operated as "black boxes" – their internal workings often mysterious even to their creators. Yet these black boxes proved remarkably adept at capturing real-world relationships that had eluded more transparent approaches.

Consider image recognition. Traditional computer vision systems tried to explicitly define features like edges, corners, and shapes, then build up recognition from these building blocks. This approach made intuitive sense and was easy to understand, but it failed to handle the complexity of real-world images. Deep networks, in contrast, learn their own features from the ground up. When researchers examined the layers of successful vision networks, they found something remarkable: the networks had discovered their own hierarchy of visual features, from simple edges in early layers to complex object parts in deeper layers.

The parallel with human visual processing is striking. Neuroscience research shows that our visual cortex also processes information hierarchically, starting with simple features and building up to complex recognition. Just as we can't explain exactly how we recognize a friend's face in a crowd, the deep learning system's process resists simple explanation. Yet both consistently work with remarkable accuracy.

In medical diagnosis, this parallel becomes even more profound. Consider dermatology, where deep learning systems have achieved expert-level accuracy in identifying skin cancers. Traditional attempts to codify diagnosis into explicit rules struggled because the visual patterns are so subtle and varied. Expert dermatologists develop their diagnostic skill through years of experience, building an intuition they often can't fully verbalize. When asked how they identify a particular type of melanoma, they might say "I just know it when I see it."

Deep learning systems appear to develop similar pattern recognition capabilities. A 2017 study in Nature showed a deep learning system matching board-certified dermatologists in identifying skin cancer from photographs. The system learned patterns from over 129,000 clinical images, developing its own "intuition" for identifying suspicious lesions. Like human experts, it can spot subtle indicators that defy simple explanation but consistently predict malignancy.

The story of protein folding provides another compelling example. For decades, scientists tried to create explicit rules for predicting how proteins fold into their three-dimensional shapes. Despite understanding the basic physics involved, the complexity of the folding process made accurate prediction nearly impossible. DeepMind's AlphaFold system approached the problem differently. Rather than trying to encode the rules of protein folding, it learned patterns from databases of known protein structures. The result was breakthrough accuracy in predicting protein structures, including many that had stumped researchers for years.

What makes these successes particularly intriguing is how they mirror human expertise. A master chef can't fully explain how they know when a dish is perfectly seasoned. An experienced mechanic might diagnose an engine problem from subtle sounds that defy verbal description. A skilled radiologist often spots abnormalities in X-rays before they can articulate what exactly caught their attention. In each case, expertise manifests as pattern recognition that outstrips explicit explanation.

This suggests something profound about the nature of intelligence. Perhaps the ability to recognize complex patterns without being able to explain them isn't a limitation but a feature of advanced intelligence. Just as human experts often rely on intuition developed through experience rather than explicit rules, deep learning systems excel by developing their own internal representations that defy simple explanation.

Consider how this plays out in language translation. Traditional approaches tried to encode grammar rules and word relationships explicitly. Modern neural machine translation systems, in contrast, learn patterns directly from millions of examples. Like human translators, they develop an "intuition" for how languages correspond. They can handle idioms, context-dependent meanings, and subtle nuances that resist rule-based description.

The power of this approach becomes clear in areas where traditional AI struggled. In speech recognition, rule-based systems couldn't handle the infinite variations in human speech, accents, and background noise. Deep learning systems, like human listeners, learn to recognize patterns in the acoustic signal that are too complex to specify explicitly. They achieve human-level accuracy not by following predefined rules but by developing their own internal representations of speech patterns.

What made this discovery even more intriguing was how it emerged from chaos. Each time researchers trained a network, they started with random weights – essentially scrambling all the connections. Traditional engineering wisdom would have predicted disaster. How could randomly initialized systems consistently learn anything useful? Yet time and again, order emerged from this chaos. Different random starts led to different specific arrangements of weights, but the networks consistently learned to recognize patterns with remarkable accuracy.

This pattern repeated across domains. In playing Go, networks developed strategies that master players initially dismissed but later recognized as profound. When AlphaGo played its famous move 37 against Lee Sedol, experts initially thought it was a mistake. Only later did they realize it was a brilliant strategic choice that human players had overlooked because it didn't fit their traditional understanding of the game. The network had discovered patterns in Go strategy that had eluded human players for centuries.

The black box nature of these systems isn't a bug – it's a feature. Their opacity is a direct result of their ability to capture complex patterns that defy simple explanation. They succeed precisely because they aren't limited to relationships we can explicitly describe. This represents a fundamental shift in how we think about artificial intelligence. Instead of trying to program intelligence directly, we create systems that can learn from experience, even when we don't fully understand how they work.

What's particularly fascinating is how randomness plays a crucial role in this learning process. These networks don't just start with random weights – they use randomness throughout their training. They randomly sample training data, randomly drop out neurons to prevent overfitting, and use random perturbations to explore the space of possible solutions. Yet somehow, this controlled chaos leads to remarkably consistent results. Different random initializations might lead to different internal representations, but the networks consistently learn to perform their tasks well.

This reveals a profound paradox: randomness, rather than making these systems less reliable, often makes them more robust. It's as if the randomness helps the networks explore the vast landscape of possible solutions, finding patterns that more deterministic approaches might miss. This echoes patterns we see in nature, where random mutations drive the evolution of complex, adaptive systems.

The tension between chaos and order in these systems raises deep questions about the nature of intelligence itself. Perhaps some degree of randomness isn't just helpful but essential for learning complex patterns. After all, human creativity often involves random exploration – we try things randomly, following hunches and intuitions we can't fully explain. These AI systems might be doing something similar, using controlled randomness to discover patterns too subtle for logical deduction.

This shift has profound implications for how we think about expertise and understanding. Traditional

AI aimed to replicate human intelligence by encoding explicit knowledge. The success of deep learning suggests that true expertise might be more about pattern recognition than explicit rules. Just as a wine expert can identify subtle notes in a vintage without being able to fully explain how, deep learning systems can recognize complex patterns without transparent explanations.

This tension between effectiveness and explainability has become one of the central challenges of modern AI. In many applications, from medical diagnosis to financial trading, we must balance the superior performance of these "black box" systems against our desire for explainable decisions. Yet perhaps this tension isn't unique to artificial intelligence. Human experts often make decisions based on intuition they can't fully articulate, and we accept their expertise despite this opacity. The challenge may not be to make AI systems fully transparent, but to develop appropriate ways to validate and trust their pattern-recognition abilities, just as we do with human experts.

The power of these "black box" systems becomes even more apparent in domains where subtle patterns make the difference between success and failure. Consider fraud detection in financial transactions. Traditional systems used explicit rules: flagging transactions above certain amounts, from certain locations, or matching known fraud patterns. But sophisticated fraudsters learned to work around these rules. Modern deep learning systems, in contrast, can spot suspicious patterns that don't fit any predefined template.

A fascinating example comes from a major credit card company that discovered their deep learning system was flagging seemingly normal transactions. Investigation revealed these transactions shared subtle patterns – combinations of timing, amount, merchant type, and location – that humans hadn't recognized as suspicious. The system had discovered new fraud patterns before human analysts noticed them. Like an experienced detective who develops a "sixth sense" for something being off, the network had developed its own intuition for suspicious behavior.

In materials science, these systems are revolutionizing discovery processes. Traditionally, finding new materials with specific properties required systematic testing based on theoretical predictions. A deep learning system developed at MIT demonstrated a different approach. Fed data about known materials and their properties, it learned to recognize patterns that predict material characteristics. It successfully identified several new materials with desired properties, including some that didn't fit existing theoretical frameworks. The system wasn't following known physical laws – it had discovered its own patterns that proved remarkably accurate.

The field of drug discovery provides another compelling example. Traditional drug development relies heavily on understanding molecular mechanisms and chemical interactions. However, these interactions are so complex that explicit modeling often fails to predict which compounds will be effective. Deep learning approaches the problem differently. By analyzing vast databases of molecular structures and their biological effects, these systems learn to recognize patterns that predict drug effectiveness.

A breakthrough came when a deep learning system identified a novel antibiotic compound that works through a mechanism different from existing antibiotics. The system wasn't programmed with biological knowledge – it learned to recognize patterns in molecular structures that correlate with antimicrobial activity. Like an experienced chemist who develops intuition about which molecules might work, the system developed its own "chemical intuition."

Even in creative fields, these black box systems show surprising capabilities. Consider music composition. Traditional algorithmic composition used explicit rules about harmony, rhythm, and musical structure. Modern deep learning systems learn patterns directly from existing music. When researchers at Google developed a system that could improvise piano compositions, they found it had learned subtle musical patterns that weren't explicitly programmed. The system could generate music that respected traditional rules of composition while also capturing more ineffable qualities like style and emotion.

The system's ability to capture these subtle patterns becomes particularly clear in areas where human expertise involves significant tacit knowledge. Wine tasting provides an fascinating example. Expert sommeliers can identify wines with remarkable accuracy, but much of their knowledge is difficult to verbalize. When researchers trained a deep learning system on chemical analysis data from thousands of wines along with expert ratings, it learned to predict wine characteristics with surprising accuracy. Like human experts, it developed sensitivity to subtle combinations of compounds that contribute to wine quality.

In weather forecasting, these systems are achieving accuracy that eluded traditional physics-based models. Modern deep learning systems can predict weather patterns more accurately by learning from historical weather data. They discover patterns in atmospheric conditions that don't necessarily correspond to known meteorological principles but prove reliable for prediction. This mirrors how experienced local weather forecasters often develop intuition about their region's weather patterns that goes beyond formal meteorological training.

The parallel with human expertise extends to physical skills as well. Consider how robots learn to manipulate objects. Traditional approaches tried to explicitly program the physics of grasping and manipulation. Modern systems learn through trial and error, developing their own internal models of how objects behave. Like a child learning to catch a ball, they develop intuitive physics that works in practice without necessarily corresponding to formal physical laws.

This ability to learn from experience rather than explicit programming has profound implications for robotics. Robots trained through deep learning can adapt to situations their programmers never anticipated. A robot learning to pour liquids, for instance, develops its own internal models of fluid dynamics. Like a skilled bartender who knows intuitively how different liquids will flow, the robot learns patterns of successful pouring without explicit fluid dynamics equations.

The power of these systems becomes particularly clear in domains where multiple types of expertise must be combined. In autonomous driving, for instance, the system must integrate visual recognition, prediction of other drivers' behavior, understanding of traffic rules, and physical control of the vehicle. Traditional approaches tried to handle each aspect separately with explicit rules. Deep learning systems learn to integrate these different aspects, developing unified models that capture the complex interactions between different factors.

This integration of different types of knowledge mirrors human expertise. An experienced driver doesn't consciously separate visual processing from prediction of other drivers' behavior – these different aspects are integrated into unified driving skill. Similarly, deep learning systems develop unified models that capture the interrelationships between different aspects of their domain.

The success of these black box systems challenges fundamental assumptions about intelligence and expertise. Traditional AI assumed that intelligent behavior required explicit representation of knowledge and logical reasoning. The success of deep learning suggests that much of intelligence might be better understood as pattern recognition operating at multiple levels of abstraction.

This has important implications for how we think about human intelligence as well. Perhaps our own intelligence relies more on pattern recognition and less on explicit logical reasoning than we typically assume. The success of deep learning systems suggests that sophisticated behavior can emerge from relatively simple learning mechanisms operating on large amounts of data.

This view aligns with recent research in cognitive science suggesting that human expertise often involves implicit learning rather than explicit knowledge. Expert radiologists don't consciously apply rules when reading X-rays – they recognize patterns learned through experience. Chess masters don't explicitly evaluate every possible move – they recognize patterns that suggest promising strategies. Deep learning systems might be replicating this fundamental aspect of human intelligence.

A note to readers: You may have noticed this section is considerably longer and more detailed than others in this book. While our goal throughout has been to present complex AI concepts in simple terms for non-technical readers, this deep dive into AI's "black box" nature was essential because it reveals something remarkable about randomness. Who would have guessed that starting with random connections and using random processes throughout training would lead to such powerful and reliable systems? This seeming paradox – that randomness could be a source of strength rather than weakness – is central to our book's theme. As we'll see in later chapters, this creative power of randomness appears again and again, from how AI systems learn to how they generate new ideas. If some of the technical details felt overwhelming, focus on this surprising insight: randomness, far from being the enemy of intelligence, might be one of its essential ingredients.

Why it works better

The triumph of deep learning over logical approaches represents more than just a technical advancement. It reveals something fundamental about the nature of intelligence and the problems we're trying to solve. Surprisingly, it suggests that embracing uncertainty and randomness might be more effective than pure logic for creating intelligent systems.

Logical approaches to AI started with a compelling premise: intelligence is fundamentally about reasoning, and reasoning follows logical rules. If we could just identify and encode these rules, we could create intelligent systems. This view led to expert systems, symbolic AI, and elaborate attempts to formalize human knowledge. It seemed like the right approach – after all, when we explain our reasoning, we usually do so in logical terms.

The appeal of logical approaches ran deep. They promised predictability, reliability, and most importantly, control. A logical system, it was thought, would always produce the same output given the same input. There would be no surprises, no unexplainable behaviors. This deterministic vision aligned perfectly with traditional engineering principles, where predictability is paramount.

But this approach ran into persistent problems. Real-world situations proved messier than any rule system could handle. Take the seemingly simple task of recognizing a chair. Logical approaches tried to define chairs through rules: has a seat, has a back, supports sitting. Yet exceptions abounded – beanbags, tree stumps used as seats, artistic chairs that challenge conventional forms. Each exception required new rules, leading to increasingly complex systems that still failed to capture the full reality of "chairness."

This points to a deeper problem with logical approaches: they tend to become too specialized to the examples they've seen, a phenomenon known as "overfitting." Imagine a student who memorizes specific math problems instead of understanding the underlying principles. They'll ace questions identical to their practice problems but struggle with new ones that look slightly different. Logical AI systems often fall into the same trap – they become extremely good at handling situations exactly like their training examples but fail when faced with novel scenarios.

Deep learning avoids this pitfall through its embrace of randomness. During training, these systems deliberately introduce random variations – like occasionally blocking out parts of the input data or adding random noise. This might seem counterintuitive, like trying to learn while wearing a blindfold part of the time. But this controlled chaos serves a crucial purpose: it prevents the system from becoming too fixated on specific details and forces it to develop more robust, flexible understanding.

The failure of logical approaches wasn't due to lack of effort or intelligence. Some of the brightest minds in computer science spent decades trying to make them work. The problem was more fundamental: they were fighting against the inherent randomness and uncertainty of the real world. Every attempt to nail down precise rules seemed to reveal more exceptions, more edge cases, more situations where rigid logic simply couldn't cope.

Deep learning succeeds because it embraces this messiness and uncertainty. Instead of trying to impose rigid logical structures, it allows for fuzzy boundaries and probabilistic thinking. It's like the difference between trying to navigate a city using only precise geometric rules versus developing an intuitive feel for the flow of streets and neighborhoods. The first approach breaks down in the face of construction, traffic, and detours. The second approach, while less precise, proves more robust.

What's fascinating is how randomness plays a crucial role in this learning process. During training, deep learning systems constantly introduce random variations – slightly altering their parameters, randomly sampling different examples, occasionally ignoring some information to avoid over-focusing. This controlled chaos helps them discover solutions that purely logical approaches might never find.

Consider how a deep learning system learns to play chess. Traditional chess programs relied on carefully crafted evaluation functions and explicit rules. They played "logical" chess but often missed creative opportunities. Modern chess AI, trained through processes that embrace randomness, discovers moves that grandmasters initially dismissed as mistakes but later recognized as brilliant innovations. The randomness in training allows these systems to explore possibilities that lie outside human logical constructions.

This adaptability becomes crucial because real-world problems rarely have clear, definitive solutions. Consider driving in heavy traffic. There's no logical rulebook that can cover every possible situation – other drivers might behave unpredictably, weather conditions can change suddenly, and unexpected obstacles can appear. Human drivers succeed by staying flexible and adapting to uncertainty. Deep learning systems mirror this approach, maintaining multiple possibilities rather than committing to single, rigid solutions.

The power of this flexible approach becomes clear in rapidly changing environments. A logical system programmed to recognize cars might fail completely when new car models appear. But a deep learning system, comfortable with uncertainty, can adapt to new variations it hasn't explicitly seen before. It's like the difference between a bureaucrat who can only follow explicit rules and an experienced professional who can handle novel situations through pattern recognition and intuition.

This pattern appears throughout nature. Evolution itself is driven by random mutations, most of which are useless or harmful, but occasionally produce beneficial innovations. The immune system generates antibodies through a partly random process, creating defenders against diseases it has never encountered before. Even human creativity often relies on random associations – the unexpected connection that leads to a breakthrough, the accidental discovery that opens new possibilities.

The role of randomness in learning becomes even more apparent in language understanding. Early attempts to program computers to understand language focused on grammatical rules and logical structures. They failed because language is inherently probabilistic. The meaning of words shifts with context, sentences can be grammatically perfect yet meaningless, and new expressions constantly emerge through random variations in usage. Deep learning systems succeed because they embrace this probabilistic nature, learning patterns that include the fuzziness and uncertainty inherent in human communication.

This difference becomes even more pronounced in domains involving perception, emotion, or complex decision-

making. Logical systems struggle because these domains resist formal description. How do you write rules
for recognizing sarcasm in speech? For understanding
what makes a joke funny? For deciding if a situation
feels threatening? Humans handle these tasks effortlessly, but not by following explicit rules. Instead, we
rely on pattern recognition abilities honed through countless experiences, including many random encounters and
unexpected situations.

Deep learning's advantage comes from its ability to
discover its own features and representations through this
messy, partly random process. Rather than requiring
humans to specify what's important about a problem,
these systems learn what matters through experience.
This often leads to surprising discoveries – features and
patterns that human experts hadn't recognized or couldn't
articulate. It's as if the systems' willingness to explore
randomly, rather than following predetermined paths,
allows them to find solutions we never imagined.

A particularly striking example comes from our previously mentioned protein folding. For decades, scientists tried to write explicit rules for how proteins fold
into their final shapes. The problem seemed perfect for
a logical approach – after all, it's just chemistry following physical laws. Yet these approaches failed to predict
protein structures accurately. Deep learning systems,
incorporating random exploration during training, dra-

matically outperformed these traditional methods. They discovered patterns in protein folding that had eluded human analysis, leading to breakthroughs in understanding these fundamental biological processes.

The significance of this breakthrough was formally recognized in 2024 when David Baker, Demis Hassabis, and John Jumper were awarded the Nobel Prize in Chemistry for their revolutionary work in computational protein design and protein structure prediction. Their achievement demonstrated how deep learning could crack problems that had challenged traditional scientific approaches for decades.

The success of this approach suggests something profound about intelligence itself. Perhaps explicit logical reasoning, while important, isn't the foundation of intelligence we once thought it was. Maybe intelligence emerges from the interplay between pattern recognition and controlled randomness, with logical reasoning being just one tool among many. This would explain why deep learning systems, which excel at pattern recognition and are comfortable with uncertainty, can sometimes surpass human performance even while failing at simple logical tasks.

Consider how humans actually learn and think. We don't proceed by pure logic, carefully deducing each conclusion from first principles. Instead, our minds jump between ideas, make unexpected connections, and often arrive at correct answers through intuitive leaps we can't fully explain. Our creativity depends on this ability to make random associations and explore unexpected possibilities. Deep learning systems, in their own way, mirror this process of discovery through controlled chaos.

This insight has far-reaching implications. It suggests that building intelligent systems might be less about programming precise rules and more about creating architectures that can effectively learn from experience, embracing rather than fighting against uncertainty and randomness. It implies that some aspects of intelligence might be inherently difficult to explain in logical terms precisely because they emerge from this dance between pattern and randomness. And it hints that the path to more advanced AI might lie not in increasingly sophisticated rule systems, but in better ways of harnessing controlled chaos to learn from data.

The revolutionary impact of deep learning on science and human knowledge was further validated in 2024 when Geoffrey Hinton was awarded the Nobel Prize in Physics for his pioneering contributions to deep learning. This marked a historic moment - the first time the physics prize recognized achievements in artificial intelligence, acknowledging how deep learning had fundamentally transformed our understanding of information processing and intelligence itself.

As we close this chapter, we can see how the deep

learning revolution has transformed not just our technical capabilities, but our understanding of intelligence itself. By showing us that the most effective approaches often aren't the most logically transparent ones, it has challenged us to rethink fundamental assumptions about how intelligence works. Perhaps most surprisingly, it has revealed that randomness, far from being an obstacle to intelligence, might be one of its essential ingredients. This principle reached its most dramatic demonstration yet with the arrival of ChatGPT and similar large language models. As we'll see in the next chapter, these systems pushed the power of randomness and pattern recognition to new heights, creating AI that can engage in open-ended conversation, generate creative content, and demonstrate capabilities that would have seemed impossible just a few years ago. Their success not only validated the principles we've explored in this chapter but opened up new questions about the nature of intelligence and creativity.

References & Sources

Word Embeddings Discovery

Efficient Estimation of Word Representations in Vector Space

Tomas Mikolov, Kai Chen, Greg Corrado, and Jeffrey Dean

arXiv preprint, 2013

Introduces word2vec and demonstrates how neural networks can learn meaningful word relationships from raw text.

Word Analogies in Vector Space

Linguistic Regularities in Continuous Space Word Representations

Tomas Mikolov, Wen-tau Yih, and Geoffrey Zweig

NAACL-HLT, 2013

Documents the discovery of semantic relationships in word embeddings, including the famous country-capital relationships.

Neural Network Initialization

Understanding the Difficulty of Training Deep Feedforward Neural Networks

Xavier Glorot and Yoshua Bengio

AISTATS, 2010

Explores how random initialization affects neural network learning and convergence.

Black Box Model Analysis

The Building Blocks of Interpretability

Chris Olah, Arvind Satyanarayan, Ian Johnson, et al.

Distill, 2018

Examines how deep learning models capture and represent real-world relationships, despite their opacity.

Emergent Properties in Neural Networks

Neural Networks and Physical Systems with Emergent Collective Computational Abilities

John J. Hopfield

Proceedings of the National Academy of Sciences, 1982

Foundational work on how structured behavior emerges from neural network training.

The ChatGPT Phenomenon

Large Language Models

Picture yourself standing in the world's largest library - a vast space containing not just every book ever written, but every webpage created, every article published, every conversation typed online, every social media post shared. It's an ocean of human communication so vast it would take multiple lifetimes to read even a fraction of it. Now imagine having the ability to instantly spot patterns across all of this information - not just obvious connections, but subtle relationships that weave through this ocean of words. This gives you a glimpse into the remarkable world of Large Language Models, or LLMs, where patterns emerge from seeming chaos to create something extraordinary.

For decades, computer scientists tried to teach machines to understand language through explicit rules. They created extensive databases of grammar, word definitions, and logical relationships. It was like trying to teach someone a language by making them memorize dictionaries and grammar textbooks. The results were predictably rigid - systems that could handle simple, straightforward statements but stumbled over the slightest complexity. These rule-based systems would get confused by basic elements of human communication like context, sarcasm, or idioms. Ask one of these older systems to interpret "The bank is closed," and it had no way to know if you meant a financial institution or a riverbank, because it was just following predetermined rules.

The way modern LLMs learn is surprisingly similar to how humans acquire language. Think back to how you learned your native tongue. You didn't begin with grammar textbooks - you absorbed language naturally, immersed in a world of words. You encountered countless variations in how people communicate, from formal writing to casual conversation. You learned that "cool" could mean both "slightly cold" and "awesome" simply by seeing how people used it in different contexts. You figured out sarcasm not by following rules, but by recognizing patterns in tone and context.

This is where modern LLMs represent a fundamental shift in approach. Instead of trying to program rigid rules, researchers created systems that could learn from examples - vast numbers of examples. Imagine a child who could read and remember every book, article, and conversation they ever encountered. That's essentially what these models do during their training. They process massive amounts of text, gradually learning patterns in how humans use language. But they don't just learn simple patterns like "this word often follows that word." They learn deep, contextual patterns about how ideas relate to each other.

The real breakthrough came with the Transformer

architecture (that's the "T" in ChatGPT). To understand why this was such a game-changer, imagine trying to read a book through a tiny window that only shows one word at a time. That's how older AI systems had to process language - one word after another, struggling to maintain context. It's like trying to understand a movie by only seeing one frame every few seconds. You might grasp the basic plot, but you'd miss all the subtle connections and meanings that come from seeing everything together.

The Transformer changed everything by enabling AI to look at all the words simultaneously, much like we do. Think about how you understand language in real life. When someone says, "John told Bob that he would help him with his project," you instantly know who "he" and "him" refer to based on the whole context. You're not processing the sentence one word at a time - you're seeing all the relationships at once. That's what Transformers do, and they do it through something called "attention mechanisms."

Imagine you're at a busy party. In one glance, you can take in the whole scene - who's talking to whom, who's laughing together, who's standing apart. You naturally pay more attention to the conversations relevant to you while still being aware of everything else happening. Transformers work similarly. When processing a sentence, they can "look" at all the words simultaneously and figure out which relationships between words are most important for understanding the meaning.

This ability to process language holistically rather than sequentially lets LLMs grasp context in ways their predecessors never could. Each word in their vocabulary exists not as a fixed point but as a flexible concept, with meanings that shift based on context. The word "bright" might mean intelligent, luminous, cheerful, or vivid - and the model maintains all these possibilities until context clarifies the intended meaning.

However, we need to be clear about what these models really are - and aren't. While their output can be remarkably sophisticated, LLMs don't actually understand information the way we do. They're more like incredibly sophisticated pattern recognition engines. Think of it like a master mime performing a piano concert. The mime might perfectly recreate the movements of a concert pianist, showing you exactly how fingers should dance across invisible keys. The performance might be flawless, but there's no actual music being played. Similarly, when ChatGPT discusses quantum physics or composes poetry, it's not drawing from genuine understanding or emotion. Instead, it's recognizing and reproducing patterns in how humans have discussed these topics.

This pattern-matching nature leads to some interesting limitations. LLMs can sometimes generate text that sounds perfectly plausible but is factually incorrect

- what researchers call "hallucinations." They can write confidently about events that never happened or make up scientific-sounding explanations that don't actually make sense. This happens because they're matching patterns rather than reasoning from first principles.

This brings us to some common misconceptions about what LLMs can really do. Many people, when first interacting with these systems, assume they actually understand what they're saying, that they have beliefs, feelings, and consciousness. It's an easy mistake to make because these systems are so good at mimicking human communication patterns. But they're essentially sophisticated echoes of human communication rather than beings with genuine thoughts and feelings.

One of the most impressive aspects of these systems is their ability to adapt their communication style based on context. If you ask an LLM to explain a complex topic to different audiences, it will adjust its language and examples accordingly. This isn't because it "understands" its audience in the way a human teacher would. Rather, it's recognizing and reproducing patterns in how complex topics are explained to different audiences.

What makes these systems truly fascinating isn't just their pattern-matching abilities - it's how they generate responses that feel natural and human-like. This involves a delicate balance of pattern recognition and controlled randomness, a topic so rich and important that it deserves its own dedicated exploration. In the next section, we'll dive deep into how embracing elements of randomness allows these systems to break free from rigid, mechanical responses and produce text that feels genuinely human-like.

But before we explore that intriguing aspect, let's appreciate what we've covered: the fundamental shift from rule-based to pattern-based approaches, the revolutionary impact of the Transformer architecture, and the true nature of these systems as pattern recognition engines rather than conscious entities. Understanding these foundations will help us better grasp how randomness transforms these sophisticated pattern-matchers into something that can engage with humans in remarkably natural ways.

How embracing randomness led to human-like responses

Picture two friends discussing their favorite books. Ask them the same question on different days, and you'll never get identical responses - yet each answer feels authentic and natural. This simple observation holds a profound truth that transformed AI: human communication thrives on subtle variations and unpredictability. Our minds don't operate like deterministic machines but rather dance on the edge of chaos, where creativity and understanding emerge from controlled uncertainty.

Early AI researchers fought against this reality. They believed that creating human-like AI meant building systems of perfect precision and consistency. Their chatbots followed strict rules and gave the same answers every time - much like a customer service script read verbatim. While these responses were reliable, they felt mechanical and lifeless, lacking the natural flow of human conversation. It was as if they were trying to capture the ocean's complexity by building perfectly regular waves in a swimming pool.

The turning point came when researchers made a counterintuitive discovery. The path to more human-like AI didn't lie in perfect precision, but in carefully managed imperfection. They noticed that humans don't just tolerate variation in communication - we expect it. We find people who give identical responses to everything somewhat unsettling, like talking to someone reading from cue cards. Our brains are actually wired to seek out and respond to this controlled unpredictability.

Consider asking an AI system "How are you today?" A deterministic system might always respond "I am functioning normally" - technically accurate but jarringly artificial. Modern LLMs, incorporating controlled randomness, might say "Doing well, thanks for asking" one time, "Ready to help!" another time, or even "Focused and operational today" - each response feeling natural while acknowledging their AI nature. This variation mirrors how humans rarely give identical responses to casual greetings.

Think about how you tell a story to different friends. Each retelling varies slightly - you might emphasize different details, use different words, or adjust your tone. These variations don't make your story less authentic; they make it more engaging and natural. In fact, these subtle variations reveal something fundamental about human cognition: our thoughts and memories aren't stored as fixed scripts but as patterns that reconstruct themselves slightly differently each time, incorporating random elements from our current state of mind and environment.

Researchers began experimenting with introducing

controlled amounts of randomness into their models. The results were striking. When allowed to vary their responses within reasonable bounds, AI systems suddenly began to sound more natural, more engaging, and paradoxically, more reliable in their ability to maintain meaningful conversations. It was like watching a skilled improviser rather than an actor reciting memorized lines.

Consider a simple example: asking about the color of the sky. A traditional AI might always respond with "The sky is blue." But humans know the sky isn't always blue - it can be grey on cloudy days, orange at sunset, or black at night. Modern LLMs, embracing controlled randomness, might sometimes mention these variations, making their responses feel more thoughtful and authentic. More importantly, they might occasionally make novel connections - comparing the sky to a mood, a memory, or an abstract concept - just as humans do in natural conversation.

The probabilistic nature of language itself demands this kind of flexibility. Take the phrase "That's interesting." Depending on context and tone, it could express genuine fascination, polite dismissal, or subtle sarcasm. Early AI systems struggled with such ambiguity, defaulting to the most literal interpretation. Modern LLMs, by embracing uncertainty, can recognize and generate these subtle variations in meaning. When responding to "What do you think about quantum physics?", they might sometimes express wonder at its complexity, other times focus on practical applications, or occasionally admit its counterintuitive nature - just as different humans might emphasize different aspects of the subject.

This shift wasn't just about varying word choice. It enabled AI systems to adapt their communication style to different contexts, much like humans do. The same model could now generate formal technical explanations or casual conversational responses, serious analytical pieces or playful creative writing. Each response might be slightly different, but all would feel appropriate to the context. This adaptability emerged from the interplay between learned patterns and controlled randomness, similar to how human communication styles naturally shift based on social context.

But perhaps the most profound impact was on the AI's ability to engage in creative tasks. By allowing for controlled uncertainty, these systems could now generate novel combinations of ideas while maintaining coherence - something the rigid, rule-based systems could never achieve. It's similar to how jazz musicians improvise within the structure of a song, creating something new while staying true to the underlying harmony. The randomness provides the spark of creativity, while the learned patterns provide the structure that makes it meaningful.

For example, ask an LLM to describe a sunset ten

times, and you'll get ten distinct descriptions, each drawing from different aspects of the training data: one might focus on colors ("The sky erupted in shades of amber and rose"), another on emotional impact ("A peaceful calm descended as day surrendered to night"), a third on scientific explanation ("As sunlight traveled through more atmosphere, shorter wavelengths scattered away"). This mirrors how human writers approach the same topic differently each time, drawing from their pool of knowledge and experience in unique ways. The randomness allows the system to explore different combinations of learned patterns, much like how human creativity often comes from unexpected connections between existing ideas.

The success of this approach challenged our fundamental assumptions about artificial intelligence. We discovered that the key to making machines communicate more like humans wasn't to make them more machine-like in their precision, but to embrace the beautiful imperfection that characterizes human thought and expression. This insight aligned with emerging understanding in neuroscience about how human brains balance structure and randomness to generate coherent thoughts and behaviors.

This embrace of randomness also helps LLMs handle the inherent ambiguity in human language. Consider the sentence "The chicken is ready to eat." Does it mean the chicken is cooked and ready to be consumed, or that a living chicken is hungry? Humans effortlessly use context to resolve such ambiguities, and by incorporating controlled randomness, AI systems can better handle these multiple possible interpretations. Rather than always defaulting to the most common meaning, they can consider alternative interpretations based on context, much like humans do.

This revelation set the stage for understanding how modern language models actually generate text - a process where controlled randomness plays a crucial role. But before we dive into those technical details, it's worth noting that this insight extends far beyond language models. The same principle - that controlled randomness often leads to more natural and effective results - has proven valuable across many areas of AI, from game-playing systems to creative applications. It suggests that uncertainty, far from being a problem to eliminate, might be an essential ingredient in creating truly intelligent systems.

The role of controlled randomness in text generation

Let's peek behind the curtain of how AI actually generates text, but with a twist that might surprise you. The magic doesn't lie in perfect prediction, but in artful uncertainty - a carefully orchestrated dance between chaos and control.

Imagine you're playing a word association game. I say "coffee," and you might think "hot," "morning," or "beans." Each response is reasonable, but there's no single "correct" answer. This is exactly the situation AI faces with every word it generates. For each decision, it sees not just one clear path, but a vast probability landscape, with peaks and valleys representing the likelihood of different choices. This landscape isn't static - it shifts and morphs based on context, much like how our own mental associations change depending on circumstances.

When ChatGPT considers what to say next, it's not simply picking the most likely word. Instead, it uses a process called sampling - think of it as a sophisticated way of rolling weighted dice. Each possible word gets assigned a probability, but unlike a simple random choice, the AI uses various sampling strategies to make its selections more nuanced and coherent.

The most basic approach, called "greedy sampling,"

always picks the highest probability option - like always ordering your favorite dish at a restaurant. But this leads to repetitive, predictable text. More sophisticated methods like "top-k sampling" first narrow the choices to the k most likely options (imagine limiting your restaurant choice to the top 5 dishes), then choose among them. "Nucleus sampling" (or top-p) is even more flexible - it considers options until their cumulative probability reaches a threshold, like saying "I'll consider dishes until I hit 90% of my usual preferences."

This is where "temperature" comes in - a fascinating concept that controls how random or predictable the AI's choices will be. Think of it like a creativity dial, but one that actually modifies the underlying probability landscape. At low temperature, the landscape becomes more extreme - high peaks become higher, valleys deeper, making the AI more likely to choose the "obvious" options. At high temperature, the landscape flattens, giving even unlikely choices a chance to be selected.

Let's see this in action with a concrete example. Imagine the AI is writing a story and needs to complete the sentence "The detective looked at the mysterious..."

At very low temperature (0.1):

- Almost always chooses: "package" or "letter" - safe, conventional options

- Generates predictable but reliable text Perfect for

factual writing or when accuracy is crucial

At medium temperature (0.7):

- Might choose: "footprints," "symbol," "shadow," "device," or "artifact"

- Each option feels natural but adds different flavor to the story

- Balances predictability with creative variation

At high temperature (1.0):

- Could venture into: "constellation of clues," "dance of dust motes," or "whispers of past crimes"

- More poetic and unexpected choices

- Risks becoming purple prose or losing coherence

The sampling method and temperature work together to shape the AI's creative voice. For instance, combine nucleus sampling (top-p = 0.9) with low temperature, and you get writing that stays on-topic but avoids the most obvious choices. It's like a chef who consistently makes excellent dishes while subtly varying the recipes.

But here's where it gets truly interesting: this controlled randomness does more than just vary word choice. It helps the AI maintain that elusive quality we call "natural language." Human speech has a rhythm to it, a balance between predictability and surprise. We don't just communicate information; we express personality, style, and mood through subtle variations in how we say things. This variation isn't random noise - it's an essential part of how we convey meaning.

Consider how the same idea might be expressed differently depending on sampling settings:

Low temperature + strict sampling:

"The project was completed on schedule and within budget."(Clear, professional, predictable)

Medium temperature + balanced sampling:

"We wrapped up the project right on time and didn't break the bank." (More casual, natural-sounding variation)

High temperature + diverse sampling:

"Our journey through this project reached its destination as planned, with our financial compass staying true." (More creative, metaphorical, potentially risky)

Sometimes the AI will take what seems like a creative risk, choosing a less probable word or phrase that ends up making its response more engaging. Other times, it plays it safe with conventional language. This dance between certainty and possibility is what makes modern AI conversation feel alive. The model isn't just selecting words - it's exploring different paths through its probability space, each leading to slightly different but equally valid expressions of the same idea.

However, this same mechanism can sometimes lead the AI astray. Just as a jazz musician's improvisation might occasionally hit a wrong note, the AI's controlled randomness can sometimes generate plausible-sounding but incorrect information. This isn't just a bug - it's a fundamental consequence of how these systems work. They're not retrieving stored facts but generating responses based on probabilistic patterns, and sometimes these patterns can lead to convincing but false conclusions.

The real breakthrough was finding the sweet spot: enough randomness to sound natural and creative, but not so much that coherence breaks down. It's like tuning a musical instrument - too tight, and the notes become rigid and lifeless; too loose, and they dissolve into chaos. The perfect tension creates music. In technical terms, this means finding the right balance between exploitation (using high-probability patterns) and exploration (venturing into less certain territory).

This delicate balance helps explain both the impressive capabilities and the puzzling limitations of modern AI. It can generate human-like text that seems to show understanding and creativity, yet occasionally produces confident-sounding nonsense. It can engage in sophisticated wordplay while sometimes missing obvious logical connections. These aren't bugs in the system - they're natural consequences of how controlled randomness shapes AI behavior, reflecting the fundamental trade-off between creativity and reliability that exists in all forms of intelligence, artificial or natural.

Why previous approaches couldn't achieve this

Looking back at the history of artificial conversation feels a bit like watching old science fiction movies - their vision of the future tells us more about the past than the present. For decades, researchers tried to make machines talk like humans by eliminating uncertainty and randomness, and for decades, the results felt stubbornly artificial. Understanding why these earlier approaches failed illuminates just how revolutionary the current embrace of controlled randomness really is.

The earliest chatbots revealed how fundamentally their creators misunderstood human communication. ELIZA (1966) played the role of a therapist by simply turning user statements into questions. Say "I'm feeling sad," and ELIZA would respond, "Why are you feeling sad?" PARRY (1972) simulated a person with paranoid schizophrenia using a fixed set of responses and beliefs. A.L.I.C.E. (1995) used pattern matching rules to select pre-written responses. Each of these systems operated like a sophisticated flowchart - for every input, follow the arrows to the predetermined output.

Consider this actual conversation with ELIZA:
Human: *"My brother makes me angry."*
ELIZA: *"Tell me more about your family."*

Human: *"He's always criticizing me."*
ELIZA: *"Why do you think he criticizes you?"*
Human: *"I don't know, maybe he's jealous."*
ELIZA: *"Does it please you to believe he is jealous?"*

While this might briefly fool someone, it quickly becomes apparent that ELIZA isn't really understanding or engaging - it's just following a script. The responses are technically "correct" but feel mechanical because they lack the natural variation and contextual awareness that characterize human conversation.

Through the 1980s and 1990s, chatbots grew more sophisticated but still followed the same deterministic philosophy. JABBERWACKY (1988) tried to learn from conversations, but still relied on matching stored patterns. DR.SBAITSO (1992) attempted to simulate a psychologist by using a larger database of responses and more complex matching rules. These systems were like actors with incredibly detailed scripts but no ability to improvise. Any randomness was seen as a flaw to be eliminated, not a feature to be harnessed.

The fundamental problem wasn't just technical limitation - it was a deep misunderstanding of how human communication works. Consider how humans actually talk about everyday topics:

Person 1: *"How was your weekend?"*

Person 2 might respond with:

- *"Pretty good, caught up on some sleep"*

- *"Fantastic! Finally tried that new restaurant"*

- *"Oh man, don't even ask..."*

- *"The usual - Netflix and laundry"*

Each response is valid, and the choice depends on countless subtle factors - mood, relationship with the asker, recent events, time of day, and even random variation in how we process and express our thoughts. Early chatbots tried to eliminate this natural variation, essentially saying "If asked about weekend, respond with response template #247."

The early statistical approaches of the 1990s and 2000s seemed promising at first because they started learning from data rather than following strict rules. Systems like ALICE's successor SUPER ALICE used statistical patterns to generate responses. But they faced their own problems - they either played it too safe, producing bland, obvious responses, or went too far into randomness, creating word salad that technically followed statistical patterns but made no actual sense.

Here's a typical exchange with a statistical chatbot from the early 2000s:

Human: *"What's your favorite season?"*

Bot: *"Spring is nice weather time good flowers grow"*

Human: *"Why do you like spring?"*

Bot: *"Weather nice flowers sunny days like good happy"*

The responses follow statistical patterns but lack the coherent structure and natural variation of human speech. It's like they were trying to learn music by only studying which notes commonly follow others, without understanding harmony, rhythm, or musical structure.

The fundamental limitation of these approaches was their binary view of correctness. They assumed each situation had a right answer - either a pre-programmed response or a statistically most likely one. But human communication doesn't work that way. When someone says "I had a rough day," there isn't a single correct response but rather a distribution of appropriate ones:

- "Want to talk about it?"

- "I'm sorry to hear that"

- "That's tough - how are you holding up?"

- "What happened?"

- A sympathetic nod and attentive silence

Each response might be appropriate depending on

context, relationship, and countless subtle factors. The art of conversation lies in navigating this uncertainty gracefully, not in eliminating it.

Modern LLMs succeeded where these approaches failed because they embrace this probabilistic nature of language. Instead of trying to eliminate uncertainty, they learned to harness it. Instead of seeking the "right" answer, they model the distribution of possible appropriate responses. They understand that language is less like solving a math problem and more like navigating a social situation - there are better and worse choices, but rarely a single right answer.

This shift in perspective - from seeking deterministic correctness to managing probabilistic possibilities - changed everything. It allowed AI to handle the ambiguity inherent in human communication, to adapt its style to different contexts, and to generate responses that feel natural precisely because they're not always predictable. The controlled randomness became a feature, not a bug.

Consider how humans adapt their communication style:
Professional setting: *"The quarterly results exceeded expectations."*
Casual setting: *"We crushed it this quarter!"*
Close friend: *"Dude, we absolutely killed it!"*

Each version conveys the same information but with different levels of formality and emotional color. Early systems would have needed separate rules for each context. Modern AI learns to navigate these variations naturally through its probabilistic understanding of language.

Perhaps most importantly, modern systems learned to balance structure and spontaneity through sophisticated probability manipulation. Earlier approaches either had too much structure (rule-based systems) or too little (pure statistical models). Today's AI is more like a skilled improvisation artist - working within understood patterns and conventions, but free to create novel combinations and unexpected turns of phrase. The randomness is carefully shaped by learning, not just raw chaos.

The irony is that by embracing uncertainty and controlled randomness, modern AI actually became more reliable in its ability to generate meaningful, contextually appropriate responses. It's a bit like human expertise - a master chef doesn't follow recipes rigidly but understands cooking deeply enough to improvise successfully, using controlled uncertainty as a creative tool.

This revolution in how we approach artificial conversation offers broader lessons about intelligence and communication. Sometimes, the path to better performance isn't through more rigid control, but through a better understanding of how to manage and harness uncertainty. The success of modern language models suggests that randomness, properly controlled, might not be an obstacle to intelligence but a fundamental component of it.

As we look toward our final chapter exploring the future of AI, this insight about controlled randomness becomes particularly significant. The delicate balance between structure and spontaneity, between predictability and creativity, may well be one of the key principles guiding the next generation of artificial intelligence. Understanding how modern AI systems finally cracked the code of natural-seeming conversation helps us anticipate what other breakthroughs might lie ahead, and what fundamental challenges we'll need to address as these technologies continue to evolve.

References & Sources

Large Language Models Development

Language Models are Few-Shot Learners
Tom B. Brown, Benjamin Mann, Nick Ryder, et al.
NeurIPS, 2020
Introduces GPT-3 and documents the breakthrough capabilities of large language models in natural language processing.

Natural Language Generation

The Curious Case of Neural Text Degeneration
Ari Holtzman, Jan Buys, Li Du, Maxwell Forbes, Yejin Choi
ICLR, 2020
Explores how controlled randomness through nucleus sampling leads to more natural text generation.

Temperature Sampling in LLMs

How to Generate Text: Using Different Decoding Methods for Language Generation with Transformers
Hugging Face Blog
Thomas Wolf, 2020
Details various sampling methods and their effects on text generation quality and diversity.

Historical Comparison

A Brief History of Natural Language Processing
Jason Brownlee
Machine Learning Mastery, 2017
Compares traditional rule-based and statistical approaches with modern neural language models.

Transformer Architecture

Attention Is All You Need

Ashish Vaswani, Noam Shazeer, Niki Parmar, et al.
NeurIPS, 2017
Introduces the transformer architecture that enabled modern
large language models.

The Future of AI

Balance between Control and Randomness

As we look toward the future of artificial intelligence, one of the most profound insights from recent breakthroughs is the critical importance of balance between control and randomness. This isn't just a technical detail - it's a fundamental principle that might reshape how we think about and develop AI systems. Like a master conductor leading an orchestra through an improvised performance, the future of AI lies not in rigid control or pure chaos, but in the artful balance between them.

For decades, we approached AI development with an implicit assumption: randomness was the enemy of reliability. The goal was to create systems that were perfectly predictable, perfectly controlled. Engineers and researchers treated uncertainty like a bug to be eliminated, a flaw in the system. This mindset was understandable - after all, who wants randomness in their calculator or unpredictability in their banking software? But nature tells a different story. From the way our brains work to how evolution drives innovation, from the complex dynamics of weather systems to the delicate balance of ecosystems, the most sophisticated systems we know don't eliminate randomness - they harness it.

Consider how a jazz musician improvises. They're

not playing randomly, but they're not following a strict script either. They're operating in a sweet spot between chaos and order, using controlled spontaneity to create something both structured and surprising. The best improvisers know exactly when to follow conventional patterns and when to break them, when to build tension and when to release it. This balance, we're discovering, isn't just nice to have - it's essential for any system that needs to be both reliable and adaptive.

The challenge lies in finding the right balance for each context. Critical systems like medical diagnosis or financial transactions need minimal randomness, prioritizing consistency and reliability. Creative tasks benefit from higher levels of controlled randomness, while strategic planning requires moderate randomness to explore alternatives while maintaining logical coherence. Learning and adaptation need enough randomness to explore new solutions but not so much that they can't build on past successes.

This balance raises profound questions about the nature of intelligence itself. Is unpredictability an essential component of consciousness? When we interact with AI systems, do we want them to be perfectly predictable, or do we value the element of surprise that characterizes human interaction? The ethical implications are equally complex - an AI system making life-or-death decisions needs to be reliable and consistent, but one helping with creative work or personal growth might need to occasionally challenge our assumptions or suggest unexpected directions.

The future might lie in AI systems that can dynamically adjust their own "temperature" - their level of randomness - based on context and stakes. Like a skilled human professional, they would know when to stick to proven protocols and when to explore creative alternatives. This wouldn't be simple random number generation, but sophisticated uncertainty management informed by deep understanding of context and consequences.

We're learning valuable lessons from biological systems that have mastered this balance. Neural noise in our brains, once thought to be mere interference, appears to play crucial roles in learning, creativity, and decision-making. This suggests that randomness, properly controlled, might be fundamental to intelligence rather than opposed to it. Future AI architectures might incorporate this principle at their core, using controlled uncertainty as a feature rather than treating it as a bug.

The development process itself needs to evolve beyond traditional engineering approaches. Future training methods might optimize for sophisticated uncertainty management, teaching systems when to be conservative and when to take calculated risks. This could involve exposure to diverse scenarios where different levels of uncertainty are appropriate, feedback mechanisms that reward both successful exploration and appropriate caution, and training environments that explicitly value creative solutions while maintaining practical constraints.

Safety and reliability take on new meaning in this context. Rather than trying to eliminate uncertainty entirely, we need what we might call "probabilistic guardrails" - safety systems that manage ranges of acceptable behavior rather than enforcing strict limitations. Like a parent teaching a child to ride a bike, these systems would allow for experimentation within safe boundaries, gradually expanding those boundaries as the system demonstrates greater capability and judgment.

The most promising direction might be AI systems that master what we could call "wise uncertainty" - the sophisticated judgment about when and how to be uncertain. Unlike simple randomness, wise uncertainty involves calculated risks based on deep understanding. It's the difference between a novice randomly trying things and an expert making informed decisions about when to explore alternatives.

Looking ahead, the challenge isn't to eliminate randomness from AI systems, but to develop more sophisticated ways of controlling and channeling it. This requires new architectures that maintain coherent behavior while exploring possibility spaces, systems that can reason explicitly about their own uncertainty, and training methods that cultivate balance between exploration and reliability. The future of AI isn't in perfect predictability, but in perfect balance - systems that can dance with uncertainty as skillfully as any human expert.

The recognition that controlled randomness is fundamental to intelligence has profound implications for AI development in the coming decades. It challenges our traditional engineering mindset and suggests new directions that could lead to significant breakthroughs. The most successful AI systems of the future might be those that master the art of wise uncertainty - systems that can navigate the delicate balance between innovation and reliability, between exploration and exploitation, between the known and the possible.

The future of AI development isn't just about building more powerful systems - it's about building wiser ones. Systems that can navigate uncertainty with the sophistication of human experts while maintaining reliability and trustworthiness. This vision requires us to rethink not just our technical approaches, but our fundamental understanding of what artificial intelligence can and should be.

Philosophical Questions About Intelligence

The relationship between randomness and intelligence forces us to confront some of our deepest assumptions about what it means to think. For centuries, we've equated intelligence with pure reason - the ability to move from premises to conclusions with perfect logical precision. This view shaped everything from classical philosophy to early AI development. But as we've seen, intelligence seems to require something more subtle: the ability to balance structure with spontaneity.

This insight raises profound questions about the nature of consciousness itself. Modern theories of consciousness increasingly suggest that our subjective experience emerges from the complex interplay between deterministic neural processes and inherent randomness in brain activity. This "stochastic resonance" theory proposes that controlled noise in neural systems actually enhances signal processing and enables the emergence of conscious awareness.

Our conscious experience unfolds through a delicate dance of certainty and chance. Thoughts arise spontaneously yet maintain coherent patterns, while attention naturally fluctuates between focused and wandering states. Creativity emerges from the interaction of random associations and directed thought. Even our memories aren't simple retrievals but active reconstructions, blending reliability with variability. Our perception itself actively constructs reality, constantly balancing prior expectations with incoming sensory input.

The development of AI systems that incorporate controlled randomness may offer new insights into consciousness. Just as neural noise appears crucial for human consciousness, stochastic processes in AI might be essential for generating behavior that appears conscious. This suggests consciousness might not be a binary property but a spectrum of increasingly sophisticated ways of managing uncertainty.

The implications for free will are particularly fascinating. Traditional debates about free will often present a false dichotomy between pure determinism and pure randomness. But examining how AI systems balance randomness and control suggests a more nuanced view. Perhaps agency emerges from the ability to shape probabilistic patterns of thought. Free will might exist in the space between strict causation and pure chance, where decisions are neither completely determined nor completely random. Responsibility could lie in how we develop our patterns of response over time.

This leads to a new understanding of moral responsibility that doesn't require absolute control or perfect prediction. Instead, responsibility might lie in the development of wise uncertainty management, the maintenance of appropriate behavioral boundaries, and the capacity to learn from and adjust response patterns. It's about the ability to recognize and respect moral constraints while operating in an inherently probabilistic world.

Knowledge itself needs reexamination in this light. Rather than seeing knowledge as absolute certainty, we might understand it as sophisticated probability management. Expert knowledge in both humans and AI systems might be characterized by understanding likelihood distributions rather than binary truths, recognizing context-dependent variability, and integrating uncertainty into decision-making.

Creativity, long considered a hallmark of consciousness, becomes more comprehensible through this framework. Creative processes in both human and artificial minds might emerge from a delicate balance of controlled variation and sophisticated selection, integrating novelty with existing patterns while maintaining a productive tension between exploration and exploitation.

These insights extend to how we understand intelligence in nature. Evolution demonstrates this same interplay between random variation and structured selection. Natural intelligence, whether in individual organisms or ecosystems, seems to thrive in this balance between order and chaos. This suggests a deeper principle: intelligence itself might be fundamentally about maintaining productive instability within constraints.

As we develop more sophisticated AI systems, these philosophical questions become increasingly practical. The nature of intelligence, consciousness, and free will seems inextricably linked to this balance between randomness and control. Understanding this relationship may be key to developing more sophisticated AI systems, better understanding human consciousness, and advancing our comprehension of intelligence itself.

The future challenges in both AI development and philosophical understanding require us to embrace this fundamental aspect of intelligence. Rather than seeking to eliminate uncertainty, we need to develop better ways to work with it. This might lead to new theories of consciousness that incorporate controlled randomness, more sophisticated understandings of free will and responsibility, and deeper insights into the nature of mind itself.

The relationship between randomness and intelligence isn't just a technical question - it's a window into the deepest mysteries of mind, consciousness, and reality itself. As we develop AI systems that better manage this balance, we may find new insights into these age-old philosophical questions, while raising new ones about the nature of intelligence, consciousness, and responsibility in both natural and artificial minds.

New ways of thinking about explainability

The quest to make AI systems explainable has traditionally focused on uncovering precise, step-by-step reasoning. But this approach might be missing the point. Think about how we explain our own decisions to others - we don't detail every firing neuron in our brain. Instead, we tell a story that makes sense.

Take a doctor explaining their diagnosis. They might say something like: "Based on your chest X-ray, breathing sounds, and how your symptoms have developed, I'm fairly confident this is pneumonia. However, you're younger than most pneumonia patients and don't have a fever, which makes me a bit less certain. I'd say I'm about 85% sure, so we should start treatment while keeping an eye out for other possibilities."

This is very different from how we currently expect AI to explain itself. Today, we might get something like: "Analysis complete. 347 features processed. Confidence level: 83%." Not very helpful, is it? What if AI could explain itself more like the doctor? Imagine an AI medical system saying: "I'm seeing a clear pattern that suggests pneumonia. The X-ray shows the characteristic clouding I typically see in pneumonia cases, and the symptom progression matches what I've learned from thousands of similar cases. However, two things make me less certain - the patient's age is unusual for this condition, and the absence of fever doesn't fit the typical pattern. I'd estimate 85% confidence."

This new approach to explanation isn't just about making AI more understandable - it's about making it more useful. Consider how this might work in different scenarios. In financial advice, instead of just providing a risk score and expected return percentage, an AI advisor might explain: "Based on your age, savings pattern, and financial goals, I suggest a moderately aggressive investment strategy. I've noticed you tend to get nervous during market dips, so I'm recommending a slightly more conservative mix than usual for someone your age. The strategy I'm suggesting has historically performed well for people with similar goals and risk tolerance, though remember that past performance doesn't guarantee future results."

Or think about shopping recommendations. Rather than simply showing products with high match scores, an AI shopping assistant might say: "I think you'll really like this jacket. It's similar to others you've bought, but with some key differences that match your recent browsing patterns. I notice you've been looking at more casual styles lately, and this fits that trend while maintaining the quality level you typically prefer. The price is also in line with what you usually spend on outerwear."

Even in home security, where quick responses are crucial, explanations can be both fast and informative. Instead of just alerting about detected motion, an AI security system might explain: "I'm quite certain someone's at your front door, but I don't think it's cause for concern. The movement pattern matches typical delivery person behavior - they've placed a package and are already leaving. However, since this is happening outside your usual delivery hours, I wanted to bring it to your attention."

This approach to explainability mirrors how we actually make decisions in our daily lives. When choosing a restaurant for dinner, we don't calculate exact probabilities for each option. Instead, we recognize patterns: this place usually has good food, it might be crowded on a Friday night, last time we went the service was slow. We weigh these factors, consider uncertainties, and make a judgment. This natural decision-making process has several key elements that our new approach to AI explainability tries to capture.

First, there's pattern recognition. We're incredibly good at spotting patterns and using them to make decisions. When you recognize a friend's face, you're not doing pixel-by-pixel analysis - you're matching patterns you've learned over time. AI systems can work the same way, recognizing and explaining patterns rather than just crunching numbers.

Then there's the way we deal with uncertainty. We constantly make decisions with incomplete information. When you decide whether to take an umbrella, you weigh various factors: the weather forecast, how the sky looks, your recent experience. You might say, "It'll probably rain - those clouds look like the ones we had before yesterday's storm." AI can learn to express uncertainty in similarly meaningful ways.

We also naturally adjust our explanations based on who we're talking to. A chef might explain a dish one way to a customer and another way to a fellow chef. AI systems can learn to provide different levels of detail for different audiences and purposes. And just as we learn from experience which explanations are helpful to others, AI systems can improve their explanations over time based on how people respond to them.

This new approach to explainability also changes how we might think about trusting AI systems. Instead of trying to understand every calculation, we can focus on whether the AI's pattern recognition and reasoning make sense to us. This is similar to how we trust human experts. When you visit a new doctor, you build trust not by understanding their brain chemistry, but by seeing if their explanations make sense and their recommendations work out. Similarly, we can evaluate AI systems based on how well they explain their thinking and how reliable their judgments prove to be.

Good human experts know and acknowledge their limitations. A financial advisor might say, "This is outside my area of expertise - you should consult a tax specialist." AI systems can be designed to be similarly upfront about their limitations and uncertainties. This transparency helps build trust and enables better collaborative decision-making, where humans and AI systems can each contribute their strengths to the process.

Looking to the future, imagine an AI system helping with city planning. Instead of just producing statistical models, it might say: "I've noticed several patterns that suggest we should add a new bus route through the eastern neighborhood. Morning traffic patterns show increasing congestion, similar to what we saw in the western area before adding routes there. Smartphone data indicates many people are walking more than a mile to the nearest bus stop, which typically leads to reduced public transit use. However, there's some uncertainty because the neighborhood is changing rapidly - new housing developments might shift travel patterns in ways we haven't seen before. I'm about 80% confident this route would improve transit access, based on similar patterns in other parts of the city. But I recommend starting with a pilot program during peak hours to test these predictions."

This kind of explanation combines pattern recognition, uncertainty acknowledgment, and practical recommendations in a way that's both sophisticated and understandable. It helps humans make better decisions by providing insights they can actually use. The goal isn't perfect transparency - even human reasoning isn't perfectly transparent. Instead, it's to make AI systems that can explain themselves in ways that are useful, trustworthy, and aligned with how humans actually think and make decisions.

The challenge ahead isn't just technical - it's about fundamentally rethinking what it means for an AI system to be explainable. We need to develop better ways to identify and communicate meaningful patterns, create explanation frameworks that acknowledge uncertainty, and build AI systems that can adapt their explanations to different users and contexts. But perhaps most importantly, we need to shift our focus from complete technical transparency to meaningful understanding. This new approach to explainability could help bridge the gap between AI's impressive capabilities and our ability to use them wisely, creating AI systems that don't just make good decisions, but help us understand and learn from those decisions as well.

The human-AI partnership

Among my prized possessions is a foldable chess set where I occasionally play against advanced AI systems. What fascinates me isn't the AI's ability to win – that's been a reality since Deep Blue – but rather how playing against (and increasingly, with) AI has transformed my understanding of the game. This experience encapsulates what I believe is the future of human-AI collaboration: not a competition between human and machine intelligence, but a synthesis that enhances both.

The real-world impact of this partnership is already evident across diverse fields. In drug discovery, researchers at Insilico Medicine are pioneering a new approach where AI systems generate potential drug candidates while human scientists evaluate their feasibility and guide further exploration. This collaboration led to the discovery of novel compounds for treating fibrosis in just 18 months, compared to the typical timeline of 3-5 years. The AI excelled at exploring vast chemical spaces and identifying promising molecules, while human scientists provided crucial insights about drug-like properties and potential side effects.

In astronomy, the partnership between human scientists and AI has revolutionized our understanding of the cosmos. The discovery of exoplanets has been dramatically accelerated by AI systems that can analyze vast amounts of telescopic data, identifying subtle patterns that might indicate a planet's presence. However, it's the combination of AI detection and human interpretation that's most powerful. When NASA's Kepler mission data was analyzed by a neural network in partnership with human astronomers, they discovered an entire solar system – Kepler-90 – with eight planets. The AI identified weak transit signals that human astronomers might have missed, while the astronomers provided the expertise to confirm these were indeed planets and understand their significance.

The art world has seen equally compelling collaborations. Artists working with AI tools like DALL-E and Midjourney aren't simply generating images – they're developing new creative processes that combine human aesthetic judgment with AI's ability to explore visual possibilities. Artist Refik Anadol's "Machine Hallucinations" series, created in partnership with AI, processes millions of images to create dynamic data sculptures that neither human nor machine could conceive alone. The artist guides the overall vision and curates the training data, while the AI generates unexpected combinations and patterns.

However, these successful collaborations highlight a crucial challenge: interface design. Early interfaces often treated AI as a black box, providing inputs and receiving outputs with little interaction in between. Modern collaborative interfaces need to support a more nuanced dialogue. Consider the case of AI-assisted software development. GitHub's Copilot initially frustrated many developers because it simply suggested code without explanation. Newer versions include features that allow developers to explore the AI's reasoning, modify its suggestions, and guide it toward desired solutions. This interactive approach has significantly improved the tool's effectiveness and developer satisfaction.

The medical field offers another instructive example of interface evolution. Early AI diagnostic tools simply provided binary predictions or probability scores. Modern systems engage in a more sophisticated dialogue with healthcare providers. At Mayo Clinic, radiologists work with AI systems that not only highlight potential abnormalities but also provide comparative cases, explain their reasoning, and allow doctors to refine the analysis based on additional clinical context. This interface design recognizes that medical diagnosis is not just about pattern matching but requires integration of multiple information sources and expert judgment.

The challenge of designing effective human-AI interfaces extends beyond technical considerations. In financial trading, firms have learned that simply providing AI predictions isn't enough – traders need to understand the confidence levels and key factors driving these predictions. Some successful systems now use visual interfaces that show the strength of different market signals and allow traders to adjust parameters based on their expertise and current market conditions.

These interfaces must also account for human cognitive limitations and biases. Research in aviation safety has shown that pilots can become overwhelmed when AI systems provide too much information during critical situations. Successful cockpit interfaces now focus on providing relevant information at the right time, allowing for quick human oversight while maintaining safety. This principle – that more information isn't always better – is crucial for effective human-AI collaboration.

This partnership draws its power from the complementary nature of human and artificial minds. Human intelligence excels at:

- Abstract reasoning and conceptual understanding

- Drawing insights from limited data

- Applying common sense and context

- Making creative leaps

- Understanding ethical implications

- Forming meaningful questions

While AI systems excel at:

- Processing vast amounts of data

- Identifying subtle patterns

- Maintaining consistent focus

- Exploring multiple possibilities simultaneously

- Working without fatigue

- Making precise calculations

The magic happens when these capabilities combine – not in a simple division of labor, but in a dynamic interplay that enhances both partners. Consider how this works in medical diagnosis. AI systems can analyze thousands of medical images to identify potential issues, while human doctors integrate this information with patient history, symptoms, and broader medical context to make more informed decisions. Neither partner solely decides; neither solely analyzes. Instead, they engage in a collaborative dance of insight and judgment.

At Stanford University, computer science courses now use AI teaching assistants that can provide immediate feedback on coding assignments while human instructors focus on conceptual understanding and problem-solving strategies. The AI handles routine tasks and provides immediate feedback, while teachers focus on developing critical thinking skills and fostering creativity. Humans need to learn not just how to use AI tools, but how to think alongside AI systems – how to recognize their strengths and limitations, how to probe their suggestions effectively, and how to combine their insights with human judgment.

This partnership model also addresses many concerns about AI safety and ethics. Rather than trying to make AI systems perfectly safe and ethical in isolation, we can design systems that work in concert with human judgment. In autonomous vehicle development, companies like Waymo use human safety drivers not just to prevent accidents but to help train AI systems to make better decisions in complex traffic situations.

Looking ahead, the future of these partnerships will likely be shaped by advances in interface design that support more natural forms of interaction. Experiments with augmented reality are showing promise in fields like surgical planning, where surgeons can interact with AI-generated 3D models through gesture and voice while maintaining sterile conditions. Research in brain-computer interfaces suggests future possibilities for even more direct forms of collaboration, though these raise important ethical and practical questions.

The workplace of the future might be transformed by interfaces that adapt to individual working styles and expertise levels. Imagine an architectural design system that learns how different designers think and work, adjusting its suggestions and interaction style accordingly. Or consider a scientific research platform that can shift between high-level conceptual discussions and detailed technical analysis based on the researcher's needs at that moment.

The key to successful human-AI partnership lies not in trying to make AI more human-like or in forcing humans to think like computers, but in creating synergies that allow both to operate at their best. Like a well-choreographed dance, each partner brings their unique strengths to create something greater than either could achieve alone. The goal isn't to create AI that can replace human intelligence, but to develop AI that can help humanity reach new heights of achievement and understanding.

The future might belong not to artificial intelligence alone, but to this hybrid intelligence that combines the best of both worlds. The challenge ahead lies in realizing this vision – in designing systems, developing methodologies, and creating frameworks that support genuine human-AI collaboration. This isn't just a technical challenge but a human one, requiring us to rethink not just how we build AI systems, but how we as humans can grow and adapt to work with these new partners in thinking. In this partnership lies the potential not just for solving current challenges, but for discovering new questions and possibilities we haven't yet imagined.

References & Sources

Control-Randomness Balance

The Balance of AI: Between Structure and Chaos
Melanie Mitchell
Artificial Life, 2019
Explores the critical balance between deterministic control and beneficial randomness in AI systems.

Intelligence Philosophy

The Biological Mind: How Brain, Body, and Environment Collaborate to Make Us Who We Are
Alan Jasanoff
Basic Books, 2018
Examines modern perspectives on intelligence, challenging traditional computational views of mind and cognition.

New Explainability Paradigms

Beyond Explainable AI: Rethinking Transparency in Intelligent Systems
Finale Doshi-Velez and Been Kim
Communications of the ACM, 2022
Presents evolving approaches to AI explainability that move beyond simple rule-based explanations.

Human-AI Collaboration

Human-Centered Artificial Intelligence
Ben Shneiderman
Oxford University Press, 2022
Discusses frameworks for effective human-AI partnerships and practical case studies of successful collaborations.

Cognitive Science Perspective

Mind in Motion: How Action Shapes Thought

Barbara Tversky

Basic Books, 2019

Provides insights into human cognition that inform the development of more effective AI systems.

Epilogue: The perfect imperfection

As we reach the end of our journey through the surprising role of randomness in artificial intelligence, we find ourselves at a profound realization: the quest for perfect control and complete explainability may have been misguided all along. Just as a perfectly ordered crystal lacks the rich complexity of a living cell, an AI system built purely on deterministic rules lacks the adaptability and insight that emerge when we embrace uncertainty.

Throughout this book, we've seen how the greatest breakthroughs in AI came not from building more rigid logical systems, but from learning to dance with randomness. From the neural noise in our brains to the controlled chaos in large language models, uncertainty isn't a bug to be eliminated—it's a feature to be harnessed.

This insight carries implications far beyond artificial intelligence. In our daily lives, we often strive for perfect control, complete understanding, and absolute certainty. Yet nature teaches us that the most robust and adaptive systems maintain a delicate balance between order and chaos. A forest isn't planned with mathematical precision—it emerges from countless random interactions, yet achieves a stability that no human-designed garden can match.

The success of modern AI systems offers us a powerful lesson in humility. When we stopped insisting that every decision be traceable and explainable, when we allowed our models to discover patterns we couldn't fully comprehend, we achieved results that surpassed our expectations. This doesn't mean abandoning the pursuit of understanding—rather, it means expanding our notion of what understanding means.

Perhaps true intelligence, whether artificial or human, isn't about achieving perfect clarity, but about developing comfort with ambiguity. It's about knowing when to analyze and when to intuit, when to control and when to let go. The future of AI lies not in creating flawless logical machines, but in building systems that can navigate uncertainty as skillfully as they process facts.

As we look to the future, the partnership between humans and AI will likely follow this principle. Instead of seeking to replace human intuition with mechanical precision, we might focus on combining the best of both worlds—human creativity and judgment enhanced by

AI's ability to process vast amounts of information and recognize subtle patterns.

The perfect imperfection of randomness reminds us that sometimes, the path to better solutions lies not in tightening our grip, but in loosening it. In embracing uncertainty, we don't admit defeat—we open ourselves to possibilities that rigid thinking could never imagine.

As you close this book, consider that the next great breakthrough in AI might not come from more processing power or bigger datasets, but from an even deeper understanding of how to balance structure and randomness, control and chaos, explanation and exploration. And perhaps this insight might change not just how we build artificial intelligence, but how we think about intelligence itself.

In the end, the story of randomness in AI teaches us that imperfection isn't just acceptable—it's essential. In this truth lies both challenge and comfort: we need not be perfect to be powerful, nor fully explicable to be effective. Sometimes, the most beautiful solutions emerge from embracing the perfect imperfection of uncertainty.

Fang Li

Dec, 2024

Epilogue

Glossary of Terms

Artificial Intelligence (AI) The field of study focused on creating machines capable of performing tasks that typically require human intelligence.

Artificial General Intelligence (AGI) Hypothetical AI systems that possess human-level intelligence across a wide range of tasks and domains, including learning, reasoning, problem-solving, and creativity.

Bayesian Reasoning A probabilistic approach to reasoning that involves updating beliefs based on new evidence, starting with prior beliefs and incorporating new information to arrive at updated, or posterior beliefs.

"Black Box" Systems AI systems, particularly deep learning models, whose internal workings are difficult to explain, even though their outputs may be accurate and useful.

Chaos Theory The study of complex systems that exhibit sensitive dependence on initial conditions, where small changes can lead to drastically different outcomes. This theory emphasizes the inherent unpredictability of certain systems, such as weather patterns.

Contextual Embeddings Sophisticated word representations in language models that take into account the surrounding words and sentences, recognizing that a word's meaning can change depending on its context.

Controlled Randomness The use of random processes in AI systems, but within carefully defined parameters or constraints to enhance creativity, flexibility, and adaptability.

Deep Learning A subfield of AI focused on training artificial neural networks with multiple layers (hence "deep") to learn complex patterns from vast amounts of data.

Deterministic System A system in which outcomes are fully predictable based on a set of predefined rules and conditions, leaving no room for randomness or uncertainty.

Emergent Intelligence Intelligence that arises from the interactions of individual components within a system, often in unexpected or unpredictable ways, without being explicitly programmed. Examples include ant colony behavior, the formation of complex weather patterns, and certain capabilities in deep learning models.

Explainability in AI The ability to understand and explain the reasoning behind an AI system's decisions or outputs, crucial for building trust and ensuring responsible use of AI.

Expert Systems Early AI systems that attempted to capture the knowledge and reasoning of human experts through a set of rules and decision trees. These systems often struggled with the complexity and uncertainty of real-world problems.

Hidden Markov Model (HMM) A statistical model used to analyze sequential data, where the underlying states are hidden, but can be inferred from observable outputs or emissions. Widely applied in speech recognition, DNA analysis, and other fields.

Large Language Models (LLMs) Powerful AI systems trained on massive amounts of text data, capable of generating human-like text, translating languages, writing different kinds of creative content, and answering questions in an informative way.

Neural Networks Computational models inspired by the structure and function of the human brain, consisting of interconnected nodes (neurons) that process information. The connections between nodes have weights, which are adjusted during training to enable the network to learn patterns from data.

Neural Noise Random fluctuations in neural activity in the brain, once thought to be irrelevant, but now recognized as potentially important for learning, creativity, and decision-making.

Probabilistic Thinking A way of thinking that acknowledges uncertainty and considers the likelihood of different outcomes. This approach involves assigning probabilities to events and updating those probabilities as new information becomes available.

Random Initialization The process of assigning random values to the weights of connections in a neural network at the beginning of training. This randomness helps the network explore different parts of the solution space and avoid getting stuck in local optima.

Sampling in Text Generation Techniques used by LLMs to generate text, where the AI assigns probabilities to different words and then selects words based on those probabilities. Different sampling methods control the randomness and creativity of the generated text.

Stochastic Resonance A phenomenon where adding a certain amount of random noise to a system actually improves its ability to process information or detect weak signals. This concept has been applied to explain how neural noise in the brain might contribute to cognitive function.

Template Matching An early AI approach that involved comparing input data to a set of predefined templates or patterns to make decisions. This approach proved brittle and struggled with variations in real-world data.

Temperature in AI A parameter used in text generation that controls how random or predictable the AI's choices will be. Higher temperatures lead to more diverse and creative output but also increase the risk of generating nonsensical text.

Transformer Architecture A neural network architecture that uses attention mechanisms to process information in parallel, allowing for more sophisticated and context-aware language understanding and generation.

Uncertainty The lack of complete knowledge about an event or situation. In AI, uncertainty is often represented using probabilities.

"Wise Uncertainty" in AI The ability of an AI system to make informed judgments about when and how to be uncertain, similar to how human experts use their experience and intuition to handle complex situations.

Word Embeddings Representations of words as dense vectors of numbers, where words with similar meanings have similar vectors. These embeddings allow AI systems to capture semantic relationships between words.

Word2Vec An algorithm that learns word embeddings by training a neural network to predict a word given its surrounding context.